Forced into Genocide

Armenian Studies Series
Gerard J. Libaridian, editor

The Armenian Studies series promotes the study of early modern and contemporary Armenian society. The series pays special attention to developments within Armenian society, the society's interactions with external forces, and the effects of modernization on the Armenian people.

Titles in this series include:

Out of My Great Sorrows

Hrant Dink

Sacred Justice

The Grandchildren

The Armenians in the Medieval Islamic World (Volume 1)

The Armenians in the Medieval Islamic World (Volume 2)

The Armenians in the Medieval Islamic World (Volume 3)

Crime of Numbers

A Perfect Injustice

Armenian Organization and Ideology under Ottoman Rule

Cultivating Nationhood in Imperial Russia

The Armenian Genocide

The Pain of Knowledge

Looking Backward, Moving Forward

Taking Lives

Armenian Americans

Resistance and Revenge

Forced into Genocide

Memoirs of an Armenian Soldier in the Ottoman Turkish Army

Yervant N. Alexanian

Edited by **Adrienne G. Alexanian**

With an introduction by Sergio La Porta
and a foreword by Israel W. Charny

Routledge
Taylor & Francis Group

LONDON AND NEW YORK

First published 2017 by Transaction Publishers

Published 2017 by Routledge
2 Park Square, Milton Park, Abingdon, Oxon OX14 4RN
711 Third Avenue, New York, NY 10017, USA

Routledge is an imprint of the Taylor & Francis Group, an informa business

ISBN: 978-1-4128-6552-4 (hbk)

Library of Congress Control Number: 2016055997

Praise for *Forced into Genocide*

"One of the biggest hurdles to being able to truly understand history to create simple contrasts and simplify things that render everything in black and white. All of the living that occurs in the gray area gets lost. The life story you have before you of Yervant (Edward) Alexanian belongs to that gray area that cannot be visible within this simplification but should not be neglected at all if you want to grasp the enormity of human catastrophe. It is usually stated that the Armenians who were conscripted into military service were exterminated first but this causes us to forget the story of the hundreds of Armenians, like Yervant (Edward) Alexanian, who served in the Ottoman army battling through to the end of the war. Hundreds of other Armenians, like Yervant, served in the Ottoman army and fought until the end, even bestowed medals for their bravery during a period when their close friends, relatives, and family members were exterminated. Reading about Yervant's story is an inescapable part of understanding another kind of suffering; the suffering of survivors."

—Dr. Taner Akçam, Clark University, author of
A Shameful Act: The Armenian Genocide and the Question of Turkish Responsibility

"Many accounts have been written about the Armenian Genocide, which marked its centennial last year and constitutes the darkest period in the history of the Armenian people. The story of Yervant Alexanian, originally of the city of Sivas, tells the unique and compelling tale of a boy whose conscription into the Ottoman Army ultimately saved him from the fate of fifty-one of his relatives, all of whom perished in the Genocide. *Forced into Genocide* lovingly memorializes the fate of a family and a community and adds yet another incredible chapter to the history of the Genocide. This book is moving, uplifting, and richly detailed and is a gift to the Armenian community and, indeed, humanity."

—Dr. Vartan Gregorian, president, The Carnegie Corporation

§§§

"Yervant Alexanian's story of survival offers a unique glimpse into the oft-forgotten lives and experiences of Armenians who were torn from their families and conscripted into the Ottoman Turkish Army during the Armenian Genocide. Alexanian's first-person account sheds light on this tragic moment in history—the first genocide of the twentieth century. This memoir serves as an important contribution to the body of historical accounts of the Armenian Genocide."

—The Honorable Frank Pallone, Jr.

§§§

"The story of Yervant Alexanian provides significant insight into not only the tragedy of the Armenians who lost their lives during the Genocide but also, very importantly, it tells us the forgotten stories of Armenians who served in the World War I Ottoman Army. As disturbing as Alexanian's story is, it gives us a rare glimpse of another facet of the Genocide."

—Eric Bogosian, author of *Operation Nemesis*

§§§

"Yervant Alexanian has left us a much-needed inside account of the Genocide period. As such a witness, he painstakingly works to debunk the alibis, myths, and outright falsehoods long promoted by Turkey to deny the facts of the Armenian Genocide. Unforgettable is the way Alexanian provides humanizing portraits—not only of the Armenian victims but also those in Ottoman Empire who played roles as agents of mercy or death. His story is long overdue."

—Andrew Goldberg, executive producer, *The Armenian Genocide*

Table of Contents

Table of Images

Acknowledgments

Translations from Armenian: Simon Beugekian (in collaboration with Adrienne G. Alexanian)

Editor: Adrienne G. Alexanian

Translations from Ottoman Turkish: Garabet Moumdjian

Coordinator: Christopher Zakian

Consultant: Gerard Libaridian

Foreword

Every memoir of an eyewitness and survivor of a genocide touches one's heart deeply, and Yervant (Edward) Alexanian's memoir is certainly one of these. At the same time, it is an unusual account—the first I have ever seen—of an Armenian who survives the terrible killing of his people while continuing to serve in the Turkish Army! (I have seen a few reports of Jews who remained alive in the German Army during the Holocaust), and we learn there were others like him.

See also the translator's thoughtful preface asking how these survivors could do so. This memoir is also unusually rich in the generous collection of photographs of the time which are not only interesting but also in themselves powerful reminders of the everyday people, like all of us, who perished in the Armenian Genocide. It also presents a rich array of actual documents that make one feel closer to the actual times of the events and the realness of the people.

Thank you, daughter of the deceased survivor, for publishing this special memoir.

Israel W. Charny

Introduction

Mr. Yervant Alexanian's memoir provides a rare glimpse into the life of a survivor of the Armenian Genocide. He did not march through the desert and survive the concentration camps; rather, his memoir tells the story of a young man who survived through serving in the Ottoman Army. Alexanian's life (1895–1983) spanned one of the most trying times for Armenians. As he himself notes, he was born in the course of the Hamidian Massacres of 1894–1896 in the city of Sebastia (Sepastia), modern-day Sivas in the Republic of Turkey. Those massacres claimed the lives of approximately 200,000 people. According to Alexanian, the trauma of those massacres also claimed the life of his father who died in 1896 at the age of 42. His mother, Hunazant, was widowed and left with the task of raising eight children, the youngest of whom was Yervant. As Alexanian grew up, most of his immediate family dispersed and headed to the United States, while he was eventually drafted into the Ottoman Army. An indispensable member of his company due to an ability to play the bugle, Alexanian miraculously survived the atrocities that claimed fifty-one members of his family, including his mother and one of his brothers. Alexanian's life need not be summarized here, but I will seek to briefly put the events that Alexanian witnessed and experienced within an historical context for those who may be unfamiliar with the history of the Armenian Genocide as well as address the difficult question of the value of a memoir as a source for historical research.

One of the frequent questions that arises when studying the genocide of a population is why did the victims not see it coming? Some did and managed to escape; others, although prescient, were unable or unwilling for financial, political, or personal reasons to abandon their homeland. We must also remember that while in hindsight all the indicators seem to be clear and the destruction of the Armenian population of Anatolia, predictable, in the moment, it is often difficult to discern the direction events will take. The Armenian Genocide did not occur in a vacuum nor was it the inevitable culmination of ever increasing Turkish aggression and hostility against Armenians; rather, it unfolded within the complex and often contradictory historical context surrounding the onset of modernity.

There had probably never been a better time to be an Armenian in the Ottoman Empire than the 1850s and 1860s, at least if one were of the upper middle class in the urban centers of Constantinople (modern, Istanbul) or Smyrna (modern, Izmir). Both internal factors and external powers had encouraged the Sublime Porte or Ottoman administration to issue a series of reforms during the course of the nineteenth century collectively known as Tanzimat. Among other goals, these decrees sought to strengthen the Empire and appeal to European powers by insuring the rights of every Ottoman citizen, fostering public education, encouraging economic production and manufacturing, facilitating internal transportation, and regulating taxation. Although the efficacy of these reforms has been debated, they certainly gave the impression—especially to the ethnoreligious minorities of the Empire who had not enjoyed secured right until then—that the Empire was modernizing and improving.

An Armenian middle class had emerged in urban centers throughout the Empire and with the leisure time their new wealth afforded, a market for literature and entertainment appeared. Modern Western Armenian broke free from its domestic boundaries and flourished as the language of a literary cultural elite. European works were translated into Armenian, poets and novelists played with varying styles from Romanticism to Realism—the renowned poet Daniel Varuzhan hailed from Sivas; playwrights produced dramas in the Armenian and Ottoman theaters; entrepreneurs founded newspapers and journals across Ottoman lands, including two in the town of Sivas in the early twentieth century; while in the bourgeoning number of cafes one could hear conversations in a host of languages including Arabic, Armenian, French, Greek, Italian, Ladino, and Turkish. In his memoir, Alexanian notes the diversity of the population of Sivas and the numerous houses of worship it contained.

This period of cultural efflorescence is known as the Armenian "Awakening" (*Zart'onk'*) and also comprised an Armenian self-examination of their own history, language, and literature as well as a development in political awareness. The non-Muslim population of the Ottoman Empire was organized and administered according to ethnoreligious communities, known as *millets*, that were headed by the senior religious figure of that community. Thus, the representative of the Armenian Apostolic community was the Patriarch of Constantinople. The reforms and movements within the Armenian community, such as the promulgation of a constitution for the Armenian millet, weakened the power of the ecclesiastical hierarchy and reflected the rising significance of the laity in the community's political life as an Armenian economic and cultural elite arose. Prominent Armenians held sensitive positions within the Ottoman government, such as superintendent of the imperial mint, owned and operated gunpowder and paper mills, and were prominent architects to the court. The middle class engaged in various trades, small businesses, and artisanal crafts as well as being landed proprietors that started to flourish in many cities also looked to have its concerns voiced. In addition, Armenians, particularly young women, enjoyed greater access to educational opportunities. Alexanian mentions the different schools Armenians could attend in his hometown; wealthy Armenians from major cities also traveled to Europe to study. Both local schools and those Armenians attended abroad educated Armenians about cultural and political trends outside the Ottoman Empire.

In general, however, the reforms initiated during the Tanzimat period tended to have their greatest impact upon the residents in the major urban centers of the western part of Anatolia. In the east and especially in the six Armenian provinces or *vilayet*s of Van, Bitlis, Diyarbekir, Erzurum, Kharpert, and Sivas, where the mass of the population remained agricultural peasants, the situation was very different. In these provinces, Armenians formed a majority of the population in Van and a plurality in Bitlis and Diyarbekir. Demographically, the region was further complicated by the settlement in the eastern provinces of Ottoman Muslim subjects from territories lost to Russian imperial expansion in the Caucasus or to the Balkan independence movements. The reforms promulgated from the Sublime Porte were often not implemented or enforced, and many times bred resentment among the Muslim inhabitants of the region. From Armenian accounts of life in these areas, a sense of lawlessness and abandonment by the state had taken hold as Armenians and other ethnoreligious minorities were subject to raids, illegal confiscations of land, and irregular taxation.

The lack of a response by the local and imperial government and the deterioration of order resulted in larger migrations from the provinces and rural areas to the major urban centers of the Empire as well as violent protests for fairer governance.

The Ottoman Empire's loss to Czarist Russia in the Russo-Turkish War of 1877–1878 exacerbated relations between the Armenian millet and the new Sultan, Abdul-Hamid II (1876–1908/1909), who through the conflict also nurtured an anti-Christian ideology. Despite the pledges of loyalty by the Patriarch and community leaders, the subsequent internationalization of the Armenian question that witnessed the intercession of European powers advocating for the better treatment of Christian minorities in the Empire, instilled a distrust of the Armenian population in the mind of the Sultan.

The situation in the eastern provinces continued to deteriorate as local officials were given wide latitude in their administration and Kurdish irregular cavalry units loyal only to the Sultan, formed in 1891 to patrol border areas and known as the Hamidiye, sporadically pillaged Armenian villages. In the face of the increasing violence committed against them, Armenians began to defend themselves, forming both armed resistance groups and political parties. Demonstrations asking for the restoration of law and order in the provinces were held in various places in the early 1890s. The Sultan's response to the increased dissatisfaction and the disintegration of stability in the region was violent suppression. The Ottoman Army and the Hamidiye units were dispatched to aggressively punish the Armenians, curb their desires for reform, and weaken their standing. Along with Armenians, Assyrian Christians, too, were targeted in the killing. The pogroms, known as the Hamidian Massacres lasted until the summer of 1896, during which time approximately 200,000 Armenians were killed, hundreds of monasteries and churches were destroyed, and thousands of others were displaced. Following the massacres, many Armenians left Anatolia to escape the oppression and relocated to the Arab lands, Europe, and the United States, where they formed the early communities that later helped settle the survivors of the Genocide. It was during these massacres that Yervant Alexanian was born in the city of Sivas.

By the end of the nineteenth century, the despotic rule of Abdul Hamid II had not only alienated Armenians but also many other members of the Empire including Turks, Jews, Arabs, and Greeks. The most active of the Turkish groups was the Young Turks, a confederation of

Turkish liberals who were united in their opposition to the Sultan. Among these liberals, there was also a strong nationalist tendency. In 1908, the Young Turks succeeded in forcing the Sultan to establish a constitutional government in which Armenians participated. The establishment of the constitutional government was greeted with joy by much of the population, including Armenians and other ethnoreligious minorities. Many Armenian intellectuals and community leaders who had fled the Ottoman Empire after the Hamidian massacres returned in order to contribute to the future of the Empire.

The constitutional government soon found itself in dire economic and political straits, and the hope and expectations of 1908 proved to be too fragile. In 1913, after Ottoman losses in the Balkan Wars, the most nationalist elements of the Committee of Union and Progress staged a coup against the more moderate factions of the Young Turks and assumed power. The leaders of that coup were also the architects of the Armenian Genocide, known as the Triumvirate of Enver Pasha, Talaat Pasha, and Cemal Pasha. The ideals of the Committee of Union and Progress were based on a nationalist ideology most prominently advocated in the works of Ziya Gökalp, part of which aimed at uniting the Turks of Anatolia with those of Central Asia. The Christian Armenian element that resolutely remained entrenched between them was seen as an obstacle to the successful accomplishment of that dream.

With hopes of imperial restoration and expansion, Enver Pasha completed a secret alliance with Germany to join the Central Powers and in October 1914 the Ottoman Empire formally entered the war. Although Armenians had served in the military during the Tanzimat period, enlistment had been limited and promotion subject to discriminatory restrictions. The parliament had decreed in 1910 that all members of the Empire were to be conscripted for military service, and Armenians served in the Ottoman Army in the Balkan Wars of 1912–1913; they were now conscripted for World War I. In December 1914, Enver Pasha personally led the campaign in eastern Anatolia and the Caucasus. Although the offensive began promisingly, in January 1915, he was badly defeated at the battle of Sarikamish and returned back to Constantinople. In order to divert responsibility for his humiliating defeat, he blamed the Armenians of treasonous activities. A matter that remains unclear and debated among scholars of the Armenian Genocide is whether the idea of the extermination of the Armenian population as "the solution" to the Armenian question was first formulated following Enver's return to the capital or whether the Triumvirate had already decided to put such a policy into place but were waiting for an opportune moment.

Regardless of when the initial plan for the deportations and massacres was envisioned, matters escalated in the next months. Armenian and European schools were closed to serve as military barracks and infirmaries. In February 1915, Armenians serving in the Ottoman Army were disarmed and used for labor. Alexanian was one of those who served in a labor division of the Ottoman Army. He details how as a conscript, he and others worked sewing uniforms for the soldiers. When the Armenian conscripts of these battalions were also ordered to be killed, Alexanian survived through the chance ability of being able to blow a bugle, a service required in the division. Soon after the disarmament of Armenian soldiers, the general Armenian populace was required to surrender their arms, an order often used as a pretext for the arrest and imprisonment of members of the community.

At the beginning of April 1915, Cemal Pasha, after earlier consultation with Enver and Talaat, ordered the deportations of the Armenians of Zeytun and Marash. On April 24 of that year, approximately 250 Armenian intellectuals, artists, and political figures in Constantinople were arrested and deported. Nearly every single one was executed. This date marks the commemorative inception of the Genocide. Between April and August of that year, the Ottoman government murdered some 800,000 Armenian citizens. By 1916, the Triumvirate had murdered over 1,000,000 people and left another 500,000 displaced. The number of those killed reached 1,500,000 by 1923. In addition, the Committee of Union and Progress regime murdered hundreds of thousands of Assyrian and Greek citizens of the Empire. These acts of genocide constituted the ethnic cleansing of Anatolia.

Although the genocidal murder of peoples was not historically unprecedented, three salient features of the Armenian Genocide are the organized manner in which it was carried out, the perpetrators' use of technology, and the attempts "to legalize" its execution. The method of elimination generally followed a set pattern: Young healthy men were gathered, arrested, and marched out of town. At a short distance from town, they were shot or bayoneted. The elderly, women, and children were told they would have to leave their towns for their own protection. They were then put on death marches through the desert toward Aleppo then along the Euphrates to concentration camps like

Deir el-Zor. The telegraph was employed to communicate deportation orders, and the new railway lines transported overloaded carriages of deportees. The Committee of Union and Progress used the secret "Special Organization" (Teshkilat-i mahsusa), comprised of irregular, paramilitary units, to conduct or oversee many of the killings. Between May and December 1915, the government passed a series of laws intended to legalize the deportation of Armenians and the appropriation of their property. These characteristics of the Genocide and the degree to which so many branches of the government were involved in the organization and implementation of the policy of extermination and appropriation reveal it to be a modern phenomenon.

As is well known, the Republic of Turkey, proclaimed in 1923, still denies that the massacre of the Armenian population of Anatolia between 1915 and 1923 constitutes genocide. The word genocide only came into existence in 1944, when it was coined and theorized by Raphael Lemkin, a Jewish legal scholar from Poland, who suffered and lost most of his family in the Holocaust. His interest in studying crimes against humanity and the need for a new term to cover such atrocities was based partially on his own knowledge of what happened to the Armenians. At the time of the massacres, however, no such word existed and contemporary observers and reports struggled to define and describe what they witnessed. On account of the continued denial of the Genocide as genocide and of the large efforts expended to support a denialist thesis, much of the writing about the Armenian Genocide has been devoted to proving its occurrence and arguing for its recognition.

A negative repercussion of the emphasis on the need to prove the historical fact of the Genocide was the relative neglect of survivor memoirs outside of immediate circles as their testimony was not considered to be as valuable as evidence. The memoir, being the reflection of an individual's experience, is inescapably subjective. D. Stone remarks that Holocaust historians perceive Nazi documentation to be more 'objective' than Jewish accounts; so too, have Armenian testimonies of the Genocide been disregarded. In recent decades, however, the denialist position has become ever increasingly difficult to maintain as the International Association of Genocide Scholars, the European Parliament, the World Council of Churches, and several prominent Turkish scholars have clearly defined the massacres as genocide. Scholarship is moving from trying to establish the fact of the Genocide to exploring the historical context in which it was committed and the local dynamics that were operative at its inception and execution. In order to ascertain these dynamics, survivor memoirs are a particularly important source for historians.

Another reason historiography has avoided survivor memoirs is that they deal with an aspect of the human condition that historiography and historians are ill-equipped to handle: the emotional. Central to the memoir is how the survivor felt and, more problematic, feels at the time of writing. More than specific historical data, the author attempts to communicate a sense of a lost life before the atrocities in order to more powerfully convey the trauma of living through that atrocity, a trauma that often transcends verbal expression. The historical memoir has thus proven a challenge to the historian. Questions of motive, the accuracy of memory and the impact of collective memory, the filter of time and context, the selective nature of their contents, as well as of the inevitably partial and singular perspective they present render the memoir a difficult source to assess.

Despite these obstacles, which we may add any written source poses, the memoir is often the historian's only clue into marginalized segments of a society—women, minorities, the lower classes—whose experiences and perspectives are often ignored, dismissed, stereotyped, or simply unknown by official historiography. There are some 200 published translations of survivor memoirs. Among them only a few are by Armenians who served in the Ottoman Army, the most famous being that of Sarkis Torossian, but to which Alexanian's can now be added. In addition, hundreds of oral recordings housed at the University of California, Los Angeles, Columbia University, the Armenian Library of America, the Armenian Assembly of America, the Zoryan Institute, and the Armenian Film Foundation; there are also survivor testimonies collected and preserved in Armenia by that have been translated into English. These represent a large body of source material underutilized by the historiographical tradition. This is not to say that a memoir, even a survivor's memoir, should not be critically interpreted; it absolutely must be if the reluctance among researchers to employ the memoir is to be overcome. Alexanian's memoir is no exception.

The memoir is not the product of a single effort to construct a narrative about what the author lived through but was composed over a period of time after the events he describes. It is also clear that Alexanian wrote at a point at which the atrocities he witnessed and the traumatic losses he suffered had been internalized and processed through reflection, dialogue with others, and the political debates of his time. Usefully appended to the memoir are the letters in which Alexanian wrote about his experiences and which he sent to political leaders, newspapers, friends, and his former headmaster at the Collège des Quarante Martyrs in Sivas, Father de Lavernette. These letters show Alexanian to have been an engaged member of his community and interested in current affairs. His memoir thus was composed when he had a vocabulary and a framework in which to translate his sufferings and memories. For example, he anachronistically employs the term "genocide" throughout his text, a word that could not have entered his thinking during the atrocities. Likewise, Alexanian often reduces interrelations between "Turks" and "Armenians," although his own recollections contradict and complicate such a simple understanding of either community. An interesting case in point is that he recalls giving French lessons to a Turkish officer, Ahmet Bey, whose daughter would listen in and tease the young Alexanian with a few Armenian words she knew. In June 1915, Alexanian wrote to Ahmet to help him avoid being arrested on the allegation of avoiding conscription as he was too young, but the latter said he was unable to do anything. Alexanian was clearly hurt by Ahmet Bey's inability or unwillingness to assist him, because "he had abandoned me in my time of need." Alexanian was "saved" from the deportations by another Turkish officer, Khalil Shukri Bey, whom he knew. Shukri Bey frequented the store in which Alexanian used to work and the latter would deliver utensils to him. His account suggests that there were certain social obligations and expectations that the youth had of these men and that he was not just calling upon people with whom he was merely familiar or shared a business relationship. In the crisis of the World War I and the Armenian deportations, however, the links that united the communities were beginning to break down as Ahmet Bey's failure to help Alexanian may indicate.

Alexanian's memoir also underscores that not all Armenians were the same. He refers to the story of how Dr. Jessourian was released from prison to indicate that wealthy and connected Armenians had greater opportunities for survival. Armenians could also choose from various Christian confessions, and it is clear that the Apostolic Church did not exercise a monopoly over the Armenian population. Armenian children could attend different schools: Armenian and American Protestant, Jesuit Catholic, or Armenian Apostolic. Although Alexanian observes that Armenian families were wary of the Catholic and Protestant missionaries and their schools, they still sent their children to them, most probably—but not necessarily only—because tuition was more affordable. Alexanian himself started his education in the Armenian Protestant school of Sivas, but as his family could no longer afford the tuition, he transferred to the Jesuit Collège where admission at that moment was free. He does not explain why he never attended the Armenian Aramian School, but perhaps it was due to the cost of tuition.

Alexanian further reveals difficulties within his own family as they tried to navigate their changing circumstances. His elder brothers left Sivas and eventually migrated to the United States. The presence or absence of his brothers seriously impacted the financial situation of the family and forced the young Alexanian to become an essential source of income for his family. Tensions in the family are also evident in Alexanian's narrative. After his brother Hovhannes' marriage, Alexanian and his mother moved in with him and his new wife. His mother was hesitant to accept the move, not wishing to be indebted to her son and his new family. According to Alexanian, her reluctance was prescient as her daughter-in-law mistreated them. It was the birth of a male cousin, however, that finally pushed them to leave. Alexanian is silent on the exact reasons for their departure, but we may speculate that his aunt wanted to preserve privileges for her own son. When Alexanian and his mother moved, he reports that they went to his father's maternal uncle where they paid rent for two years. Alexanian recounts these events without any anger or resentment, although they must have been trying times for himself and his mother. As with any memoir, the above examples suggest that Alexanian's silences sometimes say as much as his words and force his audience to read between the lines.

The overall impression of Sivas one gains from Alexanian's memoir, then, is one of a city and population in transition and on the move, where old ties and institutions were competing with newer ones, and traditional life was being supplanted by modernity. It was an exciting, but uncertain period for a young man coming of age at the turn of the century. Each person who comes to this memoir will find a different object to pick up and examine—whether it be a description of the city of Sivas, the numerous historical actors who enter his narrative, the details of the organization of the deportations and appropriation of property, the network of family and personal relations, life in the Ottoman army, or the experience of emigration—and will be able to interpret them through the lens of their personal experience or methodological framework. It is hoped that many people will do so and that the publication of this memoir will also encourage other individuals and families to share their recollections of survival in this traumatic period of history.

Sergio La Porta

Translator's Preface

Historiography is the study of how history is written. It is basically the study of narratives, and how those narratives affect our understanding of the past, our life in the present, and our expectations of the future.

The study of the historiography of the Armenian Genocide is still in its infancy. After all, the Genocide only occurred 100 years ago, and serious scholarship regarding the Genocide did not begin until the 1950s or 1960s. Additionally, historiography itself is a relatively novel field. Many more decades are needed to truly understand the narrative discourse of the Genocide. Yervant Alexanian's memoirs are a new challenge to the understanding of that historiography, because his narrative is so fundamentally different from the popular Genocide stories upon which our understanding of it is based.

Lawrence Stone, the celebrated British historian and historiographer, attempted to define the term "narrative." For him, a narrative was an account that is chronologically organized; focused on a single, coherent event or series of events; is descriptive rather than analytical; deals with the specific rather than the general; and it is primarily concerned with the experiences of people and individuals, rather than the abstract history of groups and dynamics.

Yervant (or Edward) Alexanian's memoirs fit this description perfectly. Most importantly, this is the story of a boy, a teenager, a man, and his family. This is not a story of international conflict, even though perhaps the greatest of international conflicts is the backdrop of his story. This is not the story of Armeno-Turkish relations, or how they deteriorated, or why. This is not a story of decisions made in halls of power, of revolutionaries defending their nation, or of the great conflict that pitted two neighboring people against each other. This is the story of "collateral damage," the story of the millions upon millions of civilians whose lives, during the War to End All Wars, were shattered by powers they neither understood nor opposed.

A slew of academic and historical works have been released in recent years on the subject of the Armenian Genocide, commemorating its hundredth anniversary. They all have their place in the canon, and each tells a unique story of sacrifice, annihilation, and survival. However, Alexanian's memoirs stand out among them, and that is why they represent a new wrinkle in the discourse surrounding the Armenian Genocide. We have all been told that Armenian men, at the outset of World War I, were forcibly pressed into Ottoman Army labor battalions and were executed *en masse* when the Young Turks began implementing their plans to exterminate the Armenian minority residing in the Empire. However, as Alexanian's tale makes abundantly clear, some survived, and in fact, many were still serving in the armed forces when hostilities ended in November 1918. The stories of these men remain untold for several reasons. They must have felt a sense of guilt at having survived the Genocide, while their friends and family perished. Naturally, they must have been reluctant to talk of their experience, fearing retribution from Turks even long after being discharged from the army and leaving Turkey. Additionally, their experiences, much like Alexanian's, must have generated mixed feelings. Alexanian makes it clear that throughout his service, many Turkish officers, as well as Turkish civilians, aided him, befriended him, saved his skin, or at least turned a blind eye to his being Armenian. The Turks that Alexanian describes, especially those serving in the ranks with him, surprisingly lack the vicious hatred toward the *geyavours* that we often assign to the archetypical "Turkish soldier." After all, in any army, any community, there are bonds that go far beyond ethnic and national alignments, and human relationships are not dictated by governments or their decisions. Studying Alexanian's memoirs, we finally get a glimpse into the world of the Armenian men who survived the Genocide wearing the uniform of the same army that ordered its troops to rape, rob, and murder the very mothers and sisters of those Armenian men serving within the Ottoman Army.

This begs the question—how could they do it? How could they salute the Ottoman flag on a daily basis? How could they put on a brave face and go on with their duties, knowing that the institution in which they served was guilty of killing their kin? Alexanian's memoirs make it clear that he had an unwavering desire to see himself through—to *survive*. This human instinct, which almost all survivors of traumatic events exhibit, kept him going through the three and a half years he spent serving his people's enemies. He survived for the purpose of telling his story and to keep the memories within him alive. Fulfilling his mother's wish for him to survive, by association, meant the survival of his mother, of his brothers, of his uncles, aunts, nieces, and nephews that he lost in the deserts of Syria. His desire to survive was also fueled—as mentioned above—by the desire to save his few surviving loved ones from the prospect of further suffering. Ultimately, his is a story of how tenacious human beings can be, and how sometimes, the instinct to live, with some help from sheer luck and the kindness of others, can lead people not only to survive unimaginable conflagrations but also to even thrive afterward.

I would also like to emphasize the duality and universality of Alexanian's experiences, and why it is important for works like his to be read by both Armenian and non-Armenian audiences. As a story of the *Armenian* Genocide, the Armenianness of the narrative cannot be denied and is a fundamental part of it. However, as a story of a *genocide*, its universality cannot be denied, either. On the one hand, it offers Armenians an intimate, unique glimpse into their heritage and their identity and helps them understand their own history better. On the other hand, it offers all readers a glimpse into the human condition, into the brutality that man can exercise against man, and the unyielding, unequivocal will to life that courses through the veins of virtually every human being. These memoirs are about both the uniquely Armenian experience during World War I, and the existential issues that every human has to grapple with—good vs. evil, acquiescence vs. rebellion, apathy vs. active protest, and the self vs. the collective.

In addition to the contribution, these memoirs make to the history of the Armenian Genocide and to the history of all genocides, they are also important because they contain the reflections and views of a highly observant man, who from a very young age, was mentally chronicling the events around him in early twentieth century Sivas. Some of his writing is devoted to the more mundane side of life—descriptions of the churches of the city, of the people's daily interactions, of the scouting movement that was just taking shape in the city, etc. These passages cogently illustrate one of Alexanian's most important messages—that the Armenians who were deported, dispossessed, and murdered were not a "fifth column" waiting for the Russian armies to get close to leap upon their Turkish neighbors. They were simply, law-abiding, mostly apolitical citizens trying to eke out a living and live decently with their families and loved ones. These anecdotes also remind us that the great majority of the Turkish population, at the time, wasn't raring to butcher Armenians. Like in most places, Armenians and Turks were simply trying to live and let live.

Ultimately, Alexanian's memoirs offer us an intimate account of the worst years in Armenian history from within the very system, the very institutions that committed the worst crimes against the Armenian population. As such, it is a one of a kind portrayal of events, a portrayal very few of us have ever encountered. It is crucial that his story, and others like his, is told in order to paint a picture of the Genocide in its totality and to make sure that we understand it as an event that befell *individuals*, each of whom reacted differently and experienced it differently, rather than as an event that affected all Armenians identically and elicited identical reactions from them. This, I hope, will be the memoirs' great contribution to the historiography of the Genocide.

Simon Beugekian

Dedication

My father often said that "a man's legacy is his good name based on keeping his word." He lived his truth throughout the time that I was fortunate enough to be his daughter; but after reading his memoir, I realized that it was not only a core belief but also one that helped to save his life.

There were two reasons my father needed to stay alive: to keep his promise to help his childhood friend escape her prison as a servant and concubine in a Turkish home and to tell his story to the world. He accomplished the former, but died before accomplishing the latter. Telling my father's story thus became my responsibility—and my privilege.

At first, surviving the Genocide was my father's gift to whatever family he had left or would have in the future. But over his lifetime it became a gift to the Armenian community and to individual Armenians, friends, and strangers alike, through his numerous charitable works and personal sacrifice.

My father was without doubt the most dedicated Armenian I've ever known. In his memory, this book is dedicated to the members of the Alexanian, Abgarian, Dadourian, and Arsenian families who were killed in the Armenian Genocide.

Adrienne Alexanian

Armenian Population Centers in Ottoman Turkey, on the Eve of the Armenian Genocide

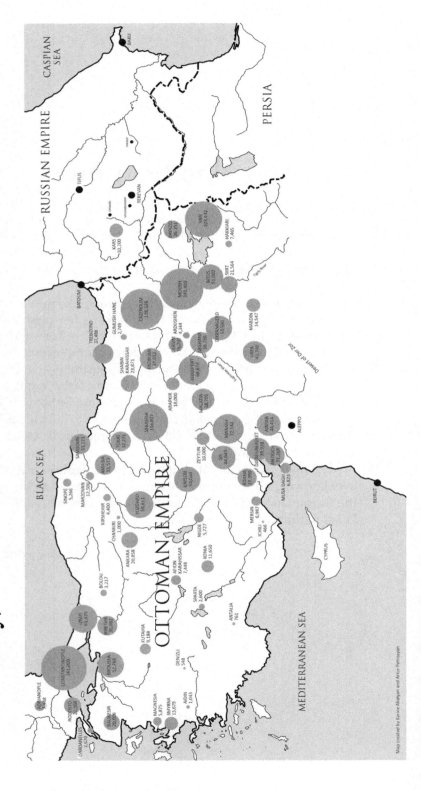

Map created by Karine Abalyan and Artur Petrosyan

This map shows the distribution of Armenians throughout Turkey in the years just prior to the Genocide; it depicts the life of the Armenian community on the eve of its death. The orange circles represent the magnitude of the Armenian presence in given localities, using figures based on the 1913 census of the Armenian Patriarchate of Constantinople. By the end of the Genocide in 1923, these centers were almost entirely depopulated of their Armenian inhabitants. Only a fragile remnant would persist amid the ruins of a once vital, creative civilization. (The information represented is based primarily on the scholarship of Ara Sarafian of the Gomidas Institute [www.gomidas.org] and the graphic visualization of Vincent Lima and Grigor Hakobyan.)

Map credit: Karine Abalyan and Artur Petrosyan.

Memoirs of
Yervant (Edward) Alexanian

The worst day of my life was July 3, 1915, when I watched fifty-one members of my family disappear over the hill. I remember it as if it were yesterday—after spending the night on the banks of the Halys River, the grisly caravan that included my family was woken and driven up the Kartashlar Yokush Hill. They were scaling the Armenian Golgotha. I stood there and watched my mother and my entire extended family climb over that hill never to be seen again. In total I lost fifty-one members of my family that day.

Yervant Alexanian

1

Childhood Early Life

I was born at 5:00 p.m., on Friday, November 15, 1895, in the Azabzig neighborhood of Sivas, in a house that was adjacent to a mill and that had been bequeathed to my parents from my maternal grandfather. My family and uncle's family shared this house. Three days after my birth, the pogroms of 1895[1] began; it was common knowledge of the time that Sultan Hamid had announced that Turks had the government's permission to fall upon their Armenian neighbors. Soon, the clerics at the mosques were repeating the government's orders and began distributing knives, swords, and other weapons to the worshippers, inciting them, filling them with bloodlust, and reminding them of their religious duty to attack Armenians. Thus, began the Hamidian massacres. As my mother once said, I was born under an evil star. As soon as I came into this world, I was thrown into violence.

A view of Sivas in the early 1900s. An Armenian church is visible in the upper left corner.

Many years before this eruption of violence, things had been different. For some time, we even had a governor who was fair and just to Armenians, but for this reason, the local Turks nicknamed him *geyavour*[2] Pasha.[3] His actual name was Rashid Pasha, and he was a member of the Ittihad Party,[4] despite his convictions and actions. During his tenure, he had even built an orphanage and a workshop that helped the local Armenians. Many Armenians referred to him as a "fine Turk."

Our house was located at the confluence of the two sections of the Halys River—the Upper Halys, which was used to power the mill and for wading, and the Lower Halys, often called Murdar Irmak.[5] The house was in the neighborhood of Azabzig, in the Kanli Baghchi district. The street was named Hassanli, and we lived right across from Bozig's butcher's shop, and the presence of that shop meant that the street was also often called *Kasap*[6] Bozig's street. Right by the butcher shop, also across the street from our house, was a barracks, as well as my Uncle *Terzi* Serop Alexanian's home, next door to Garabed Kapikian's house. Right beside our house, on the other side of the mill, was a *madrasa*.[7] The mill, which was located on the left side of the house, was a constant motif during my childhood. I would constantly hear its huge stones turning and grinding the wheat. This sound, alongside the gurgling of the water that the mill used, and the song of the water that sprang from the fountain in our courtyard, lulled me to sleep in the evenings. I could also usually hear the sounds coming from the *madrasa* on the other side of the mill. I remember that this small structure had its own minaret, and inside, a Turkish *hoja*,[8] his head wrapped in white, and wearing his *shalvars*,[9] would force his young students to constantly repeat the lessons. The children had no writing utensils, so they would simply read whatever the *hoja* wrote on the blackboard. These kids were taught to hate all those who were non-Muslim from a tender age.

This was the first house I knew until much later, when my mother's older brother, Nishan Apkarian, offered to buy the entire house from my mother for the price of twenty gold coins, so that his family and his brother Merujan and his family could live together in a two-story house. My mother agreed to the sale, and we then rented Baretenk's house, near Dr. Goghmor's house, with my older brothers Kaloust and Hovhanness. By this time, my brothers were significantly older, and as they all worked, my mother was able to stop washing other people's laundry, which she had been doing to make ends meet. We no longer needed the money so badly. Much later, when my brother Kaloust moved to Samsun,[10] and money was tight again, we moved out and rented two rooms in Godoshian's house, and my mother had to resume washing whites to eke out a living. I would help her around the house and with her work, performing tasks such as making the beds and cleaning the house. By the time we had moved there, I was old enough and was employed in diverse professions to bring in some income to the family.

§§§

As I mentioned, the house where I was born had been bequeathed to us by my maternal grandfather. My family used to tell an interesting story about him—according to legend, he was once traveling to Istanbul with a herd of oxen that he wanted to sell in the capital. He found his route obstructed by a river, and he was not willing to pay the exorbitant sum of money that would be needed for him and his animals to cross by ferry. So, he decided that they would ford the river together. Just at that moment, the Sultan was sailing down the river with his entourage, and noticing my grandfather, and amazed by his courage, called him over after the latter had swam across.

"Tell me, what would you like? I want to reward your courage with anything your heart desires."

Again, according to legend, my grandfather's response was

"I wish a long life and good health to our Holy Patriarch, your Highness!"

The Sultan, disgusted by this response, simply dismissed him.

§§§

Our family, by now, was already quite large. I had seven siblings at the time. From the oldest to the youngest, they were—Dikran, Hovhanness, Haiganoush, Harutyun, Anna and Hovagim (who were twins), and Kaloust. My brothers all worked with my father at his tailor shop, helping the family make ends meet, while my mother worked as a laundry woman one day out of the week to generate some extra income.

According to my mother, when the pogroms of 1895 began, three of my brothers—Dikran, Hovhanness, and Kaloust—were not at home when the massacres began, and neither was my Aunt Merijan. They were probably out on business. The rest of the family huddled in the upper floor, praying that the violence would soon end—a rather apocalyptic, indescribable scene. These were the first days of my life.

A panoramic view of Sivas, taken from the ancient citadel of the city, with numbers indicating important landmarks, as follows: 1, Unspecified Armenian Apostolic church; 2, The Jesuit School, which Alexanian attended; 3, Armenian school (presumably, the Aramian school that was later converted into the military workshop); 4, Greek orthodox church; 5, Perkenik; 6, Teke; 7, Saint John Church; 8, The Grand Mosque; 9, Erzinguian Street.

Suddenly, my aunt Merijan burst through the door of the first floor. The other members of the family went downstairs, unlocked the door to the second floor, and gathered there again, glad that she was safe, but still disappointed at the thought of losing three young sons. My mother was beside herself, already wailing and mourning her sons. Meanwhile, my aunt told them all how she had survived—hearing gunfire, and correctly surmising that danger lurked, she had shut her store and had tried to make her way home. Then, she had seen two Turks advancing from the other end of the road, holding guns and long daggers. Realizing that she would be lynched, she had lain on the ground and had decided to play dead. The Turks had reached her and had tried to rouse her. She had kept her eyes closed and had refrained from breathing. They had taken her coin purse, and mockingly thanking her, had walked away. A few minutes later, my aunt had raised her head and opened her eyes to find herself in a completely deserted neighborhood. She had wrapped some cloth around her head, hoping this would fool the Turks into believing she was one of them, and had resumed her walking. She had come across another group of Turks, lurking in the streets and waiting for their next quarry, their daggers red with blood.

However, the Turks, taking her for a Turk as well, just as she intended, had left her alone. Then, my aunt had basically run to the house, as if sprouting wings, and had finally fallen into the lap of her kin again, whose happiness knew no bounds, and was only dampened by the continuing absence of the young men. Just then, a gunshot was heard, very close to the house. Some of the Turkish neighbors, who had witnessed my aunt take refuge inside the house, spread the malicious and potentially fatal rumor that the gunshot had come from inside the house. Some of the Turks who were part of the mob outside went to the government and convinced the officials to give them two barrels of gasoline, and came back, with the intention of burning our house down, with us still inside. Their excitement reached new heights when they saw a bottle of kerosene inside the house through a window, as they now expected a great conflagration to satisfy their bloodlust. The screams and the pleas of my family filled the air.

Just at this moment, one of the slaves of one of our Turkish neighbors, a black woman named Dado, walked by the house, and witnessing what was happening there, ran home and roused her sleeping master, who was a wealthy landowner. Ethim *Effendi*,[11] who was a friend of my family, ran out into the street, calmed the mob, and planting his chair right outside our door, announced that our family was under his personal protection.

He was the savior of the entire family. Nothing my family could do for him in subsequent years would satisfy my mother's insistence that we pay Ethim *Effendi* back for his actions on that fateful day. Sadly, he could do nothing for my three brothers who were still unaccounted for. The wailing and mourning inside our house continued.

Three days later, as the violence subsided, government officials fanned out across the city to announce that all fighting had ended, that the government was issuing a "pardon" to the Armenians (despite the fact that the Armenians had not been the ones committing crimes), and that all could leave their homes safely, without fear of attack. Naturally, the only thing on everyone's mind was whether or not my brothers were still alive. Just then, there was a knock at the door, and all three of my brothers, together, appeared at the threshold. The return of my three brothers completely changed the atmosphere inside the house. Knowing that they would be targeted, they had hidden under a bridge during the violence. My mother spent the subsequent hours kissing them, one after the other, and sang the Lord's praises for returning them to her safe and sound.

Due to the chaotic and unsafe situation, my family couldn't take me to church to baptize me. Instead, they asked a priest who lived nearby to perform the baptismal ceremony at our home. That's when I was finally given the name Yervant. My brother Kaloust was my godfather during the ceremony.

Weeks passed, but the memories of those terrible days would not dissipate. My father was especially traumatized. He had seen, with his own eyes, the Turkish mob prepare the fuel and the torches to burn down his house and to burn him and his entire family alive. It must have been a huge shock for a man who had worked his fingers to the bones to provide a comfortable existence for his family. Seven months later, on June 12, 1896, at the age of forty-two, unable to recover from the trauma and the terror, he passed away, leaving behind a widow and eight orphans. Since I was seven months old when he died, I never knew what my father looked like. He was the oldest of four brothers, in a

A tableau created much later, in America, of the Alexanian family. Hunazant, Alexanian's mother, is at the top, followed by (clockwise)—Alexanian's brother Hovhanness, Yervant, his sister Khanum, and brothers Dikran and Kaloust.

family of eight children. When he died, my mother was so distraught that for many days, she didn't have the wherewithal to take care of me and my younger siblings. Thankfully, my sister stepped up to the plate and did what she could for me. Instead of milk, she fed me other liquids. I owe a huge debt to her for ensuring my survival. I was, after all, only a fragile newborn infant.

Life was never easy for the Armenians of Sivas during my childhood years. I recall one specific incident—I was barely ten years old, a member of a family of six sons and two daughters, five of whom were still living at home. Being the youngest member of the family, many menial chores were assigned to me, including the procurement of the household's drinking water, which I had to get a few times a week from a spring located about a mile away. I was also tasked with shopping for the family—vegetables and meat, which I would carry home using a contraption that allowed me to carry two bags, one hanging down my chest, and the other down my back. After all, the older sons of the family ran their own businesses by this point, and they weren't going to leave their work to do the shopping.

My early childhood was spent helping the family. At the time, my duties included shopping for the family, helping my older brothers in their shop, keeping the coals in our *tonir*[12] warm, etc. By that time,

A panoramic view of Sivas, specifically of the Armenian quarters of the city.

after my father's death, in order to ensure our family's survival, my oldest brother Dikran, aged fifteen or sixteen, kept his promise and became a shopkeeper, taking over my father's tailor shop. My brother Hovhanness, too, had left school at the age of thirteen, in order to help Dikran at the shop. Hovhanness stayed at the shop usually, while Dikran traveled to sell his wares, as most of his customers were farmers who could not make their own way to the shop. Much of the clothing Dikran had was bartered for essentials such as barely, wheat, etc.

Yervant Alexanian's brother, Hovhanness, and Hovhanness's wife, Anna.

At some point, my brother Hovhanness married a girl named Anna Bakalian. She was a short girl, whose wealthy family hailed from Gurin. Prior to the wedding, her father, Artin *Agha*, had promised her and her family one of his nine homes, as well as a store. He kept this promise, and my brother became the owner of a store. After the wedding, we were expected to move in with them, but my mother was reluctant, predicting that she and her daughter-in-law would not get along. After all, she would always feel indebted to her and Hovhanness, since the latter would be responsible for her financially. We moved in with them despite my mother's reservations. The house was on Bekmez Street, close to my school and to gardens, which I liked.

Soon, my mother's initial doubts were confirmed when Anna began treating us rather badly. My mother would perform all of the household chores by herself, and Anna would lie in bed and make excuses to get into arguments with her. Even worse, when a famine hit Sivas, she began demanding payment for the food that she and my brother provided for my mother, me, and my brother Kaloust, who also lived there with us. The situation was exacerbated when Anna and Hovhanness had a son, whom they named Souren. Eventually, my mother could take it no longer, and we ended up moving with my father's maternal uncle in the Bakji neighborhood, where we stayed for two years and had to pay rent. Also, at some point, we stayed with my brother Dikran for some years. Dikran had gotten married in 1912, and I remember the celebrations clearly—they had lasted six days, and a seven-piece band had constantly

The Alexanian family in the early 1900s. Background, from left to right: Yervant's brothers Hovhanness, Dikran, and Kaloust. Foreground, left to right: Yervant's mother Hunazant, with Yervant's baby cousin Levon in her lap, Yervant (aged 10), his niece Anna, and his aunt Noyemzar.

played music. I had not gone to school for a whole week, participating in the festivities. The couple had a son, whom they named Antranik.

These two brothers of mine would later go into business together. About six months after Dikran's wedding, Hovhanness had approached him with an offer—they would start a business enterprise together, alongside a third man, and would sell ethnic clothing and food. The venture was ill-fated, and within months, due to disagreements, Dikran pulled out of the partnership, despite my mother's pleas not to do so.

11

I also remember how my brother Kaloust was married. He had served for three months in the Ottoman Army and was slated to go back to supervising the coffee shop he ran, but anxious to avoid being called up to fight in case of a war, he wanted to emigrate. At the time, the entire family opposed this decision, and they made sure that Kaloust would marry—he married a girl named Nazeli Ghougassian, Nazarghan Ghougassian's daughter, who, after losing her father at a very young age, had been raised in an orphanage in Switzerland. She was a seamstress and also worked at the Derchak Hospital. However, even after getting married, Kaloust insisted on leaving, and seven or eight months later, he put his plans into motion. Alongside a nephew of ours who was also trying to escape the draft, he traveled to America. He left behind his pregnant wife, who, a couple of months after his departure, had a son and named him Karnig.

My sister had married in 1901 to Ardashes Der Kaprielian and had immigrated to America eight months after their marriage (they would later have a daughter, Victoria, and two sons, Levon and Zareh).

§§§

Before the calamities of 1915, there were many churches in Sivas. The main Apostolic Armenian church was called the *Asdvadzadzin* or the Holy Virgin. It was more than 600 years old and looked very much like the churches in Izmir and Garni, which had been designed by the same architect. The locals sometimes referred to it colloquially as the "main church." I remember how every morning, the Cathedral's bells began pealing with the rising sun, summoning the pious to morning prayers. I will never forget how at dawn, as those bells rang, people would congregate from every corner of town toward the Cathedral, where there was usually no room left within a few minutes. Each man or woman would take off his or her shoes, and after crossing himself or herself, would reverently enter the church with a bowed head. Many worshippers kept cushions inside the church, which they would use when they visited. It was always amazing to see how after Mass, all of these worshippers would leave the Church and immediately find their shoes among the hundreds of pairs that littered the courtyard outside. The Cathedral was the seat of our patriarchate. I lived to see the last patriarchs of Sivas, including the very last one, Father Torkom Kalemkerian.

There was also another Apostolic church in the city, almost as large as *Asdvadzadzin*, called the Saint Sarkis Cathedral, which was constructed on ground that had once been occupied by an orphanage that had been home to many children who had lost their parents during the Hamidian massacres.

Among the Catholic institutions in Sivas, there was a beautiful four-story stone building to house the French Jesuit priests and a newly built Catholic Church and parochial school. I myself was a student of the Jesuit school that was established in the city by these priests. These buildings were built on a choice lot between the arms of the Halys River[13] that meandered through Sivas, and I remember them quite vividly. When war was declared against France in 1914, these beautiful buildings were appropriated before the Jesuit priests had even reached Samsun[14] to board the ships that were to take them back to France. All of the statues, the stained glasses, and the altar were shattered to pieces. They used the buildings as a military hospital for soldiers wounded at the front. The cross at the top of the church building was removed and replaced by the Islamic crescent.

American Protestant missionaries also had a parochial school on a large plot of land behind the French Jesuit School. Only a few years before the outbreak of war, they built a beautiful college on top of the Hoghtar Hill. The college was called the Teachers' College, and its goal was to produce teachers who could then, in their turn, educate the local population. When war was declared, just like the French Catholics, the American Protestants lost most of their possessions, and their buildings were converted into military workshops and clinics.

Alas, all of this is now gone with the wind. I'm sure that a modern visitor to Sivas would barely discern a trace of the once-thriving Christian community there.

The great diversity of religious institutions in Sivas—there were mosques, Greek Orthodox Churches, and all the other churches mentioned above—was sometimes a source of friction and even violence. The Turks hated all Christians, and the Christians hated the Turks, but even within the Christian community, the gulfs separating the sects were huge. The Armenians did not approve of the proselytizing done by the Catholics and the Protestants, who also happened to represent two foreign peoples and, in the minds of the locals, two alien modalities of thought. A simple example of the friction caused by the foreign sects was the case of *Kiliji*[15] Zil Hampar.

How could I ever forget *Kiliji* Zil Hampar? He was an Armenian knifesmith I knew in my childhood. He had made a name for himself as a conscientious, hardworking, and professional craftsman, and he had a stall in the town's market district.

He had lost his father to the brutality of the mobs during the massacres of 1895 before even having finished primary school. He had become the only breadwinner of the family and had gone into an apprenticeship with another knifesmith. For years, he had barely eked out a living for himself and his poor mother, but he had honed his skills and sharpened his talent. Naturally, he wanted to open his own shop, but none of the established banks would loan him any money. Thus, he had turned to the Protestant community, which at the time offered low-interest loans. They were more than willing to immediately pounce on an Armenian Apostolic man who had willingly come to them, with the goal of eventually converting him. Slightly different tactics were used by the Catholic Jesuit fathers, evidently without meeting the same level of success.

So, Hampar converted to Protestantism, and soon he received the capital he needed. He was able to buy his own modest stall. Not much time later, thanks to his austere lifestyle and hard work, he was also able to build a house for himself and his family. For a time, he and his mother were able to enjoy a peaceful and prosperous life. At the time, they were neighbors of ours.

Hampar was an excessively simple, friendly, and modest man. He did not drink, did not smoke, and did not bother with politics. Every Sunday, at noon, with his Bible under his arm, he would head to the Protestant Church to pray alongside his brothers and sisters. My uncle Serop was dismayed at seeing this apostasy. "Hey!" he would call, "what did we ever do to you anyway, that you turned your back on us?" Even Hampar's elderly mother, Mania *Khatoun*, had been opposed to this conversion, but Hampar always remained loyal to his new church.

Having settled down, and owning a profitable business, Hampar's thoughts soon turned to marriage. He traveled to Gurin, where he married a certain Ms. Anna, an Armenian Protestant from that city, and brought her back to Sivas. The couple was soon blessed with two sons. Unfortunately, just as they were thinking of enrolling their oldest son in primary school, the war broke out and was succeeded by the deportation and genocide of the city's Armenian community.

During the war, Hampar quietly performed his military service by volunteering to bring potable water to the local American hospital. He stayed at his post until the Armistice.

Our neighborhood was deported on Thursday, July 3, 1915. My family and his were both deported, but as I had also been enlisted by that time, the two of us stayed behind in Sivas. I remember, on that day, we went to find carts for our families but were only able to find one, which we decided they would have to share. We wheeled the cart to the banks of the river right outside town, which was supposed to be the caravan's first stop.

After parting with our families (the story of these farewells will be retold in detail), we went back to the city. Hampar went back to his hospital job, and I went back to the military workshop at the old Aramian School, where I was stationed.

As soon as the Armistice of 1918 was declared, Hampar left everything and headed for Aleppo, Syria, where he hoped to find his young family.

There, after some time, he was able to find Samuel, his oldest son, who had miraculously survived. From him he learned just how much they had suffered. From him he learned how his wife had died of exhaustion and how their youngest child had been buried alive. From him he heard of the intolerable suffering the Armenians had experienced. More than ninety percent of the people in their caravan had been killed. I was told that after hearing his son's tale, Hampar had lost his mind and had thrown the Bible he had doted over for so many years into the mud, cursing it. Afterward, he apparently moved to Aintab where Armenians were still engaged in an armed rebellion against the Turks. I was told that he supplied the fighters with knives, but also took part in combat, and was supposedly one of the most bloodthirsty men on the frontlines.

§§§

Some of my greatest memories from childhood involve Shushan, a girl who would become my lifelong friend and whose life would constantly be intertwined with mine. I remember one particular event very vividly. It was a bright morning in May, a warm Sunday in spring. A group of boys and girls, dressed in their Sunday best, played on a wide roof lined by several poles. Some were dancing, others were jumping and running about, while yet others were kicking a ball back and forth. I was there, too, the oldest among the children, but not an adolescent yet. I sat with my back against one of the poles, silently reading, my legs stretched before me. Nearby sat Shushan, with a long reed in her hand. She was mischievously tapping the back of my neck with the reed, giggling every time. I started and tried to flick away the invisible fly, I thought it was landing on me.

Suddenly, a group of Turkish urchins appeared on the road and began pelting us with rocks, interrupting our innocent games. The other children immediately scattered, leaving Shushan and me alone facing off against the Turks. There was nothing else to do, so I rolled up my sleeves and began wrestling them. I remember my hat getting knocked off my head and immediately being trampled into the dust by one of the Turkish miscreants, which angered me even more, and getting more enraged, I pushed two of them down. Meanwhile, Shushan dropped a ladder down from the roof and signaled to me. I struck one last punch and then followed Shushan down the ladder. We pushed the ladder away and ran off.

When my mother saw my bloodied lips and nose and my torn clothing, strips of which trailed behind me, she jumped up to her feet and began chiding me. I was quite fed up. I responded without thinking—"One more year! One more year, and I graduate from school. Then I will leave this place, and go live somewhere I can enjoy freedom and peace. I don't care if I have to walk to the other side of the world!"

My mother gazed at me wistfully and replied—"Why not? I raised you alone, raised you through thick and thin, and you want to leave me here alone? Sure, why not, leave like your sister and brothers did . . . " And here, she suppressed a sob, "you're all trying to bury me alive!"

By this point, my brothers and sister had left home and were seeking fortune in America.

I was shaken and tried to comfort my mother—"Don't worry, mother... Don't worry, I will never abandon you . . . " And I crossed myself, asking the Lord to forgive the sin I had just committed.

"But why did you have to fight?" she asked, "You could have spared your clothes, and spared yourself lots of trouble, too . . . "

"But mother, they attacked us for no reason at all! You know I couldn't have left the kids to their own devices, especially not Shushan!"

She knew I was right, and I knew I was right. My behavior was not the problem. The problem lay with the nature of the relationship between Turks and Armenians in the city and the entire Empire.

Scenes from Sivas

Yaldezle district in Sivas, known for its hot springs.

The Protestant Meeting Hall in Sivas.

On the shores of the Murdar Irmak.

Kemer area of Sivas.

The water mill in Sivas.

The altar of the Armenian Apostolic Cathedral in Sivas.

Waterfalls in the Kemer district of Sivas.

The observatory of King Senekerim in Sivas.

The Armenian Aramian School in Sivas, which was later the military workshop of the twenty-seventh Division of the Ottoman Army.

Notes

1. A reference to the Hamidian Massacres of 1894–1896, during which up to 300,000 Armenians were killed across the Ottoman Empire.
2. The Turkish term *geyavour* is often translated as "heretic" or "unbeliever." It is a derogatory term used in the Ottoman Empire around that time to describe non-Muslims, particularly Armenians.
3. Turkish honorific for high-ranking officials.
4. The Committee for Union and Progress, which came into power in the Ottoman Empire in 1908.
5. "Dirty River."
6. *Kasap* is Turkish for "butcher."
7. An institute for Islamic instruction.
8. A religious scholar.
9. Baggy pants commonly worn in the Near East.
10. A Turkish city on the coast of the Black Sea, the closest port to Sivas.
11. One of several honorific titles in Turkish (another would be *Agha*) for high-ranking men.
12. A pit dug into the earth and filled with coal (or other combustibles) was used to bake bread and cook other food. It was used in most homes in the Ottoman Empire around the time of the events in 1908.

13. The Halys River (its Greek name) is somewhat of a recurring theme through Yervant Alexanian's memoirs and seemed to have symbolized his hometown for him. The river's modern Turkish name is the Kizilirmak River.
14. Samsun, a Turkish city on the coast of the Black Sea, would have been the closest port to Sivas, and thus the presumed point of departure for the Jesuit priests.
15. In Turkish, a *kilij* is a short sword or a dagger.

2

School Years

Starting at age five, and until the age of seven, I had attended the Armenian Protestant School in town, where the monthly pay was 100 Turkish pounds, which my brother paid. This was the school where I learned the alphabet, and I learned how to read and write. It was also the school in which I first was confronted with human cruelty. I remember, one day, I don't know why, my teacher decided to punish me. I was given a choice—I could either read out loud what was written on the side of a ruler or be hit by that ruler. Thankfully, I read out loud "this stick comes from heaven." I was spared punishment thanks to my proficiency in reading.

Eventually, due to the financial burden this placed on my family, I had to leave the Protestant School. In fact, one month, when my older brother couldn't pay, they summarily dismissed me from school. My mother, however, insisted that I needed to get an education, so she decided to transfer me to the French Jesuits' school, which was located

The Forty Martyrs' Jesuit College.

in a stone building on Bezirji Solak Street and which was at that point free. My mother paid for papers and pencils with the money she earned by washing clothes. Even though I was a very young boy, I also worked to lighten my mother's burden. I began attending my new school halfway through the school year, but thankfully, I was able to catch up with the rest of the students relatively quickly.

I do not know when or how the French Jesuit Fathers had come to the Ottoman Empire, where they had established schools in Sivas and in many other cities, including Samsun and Tokat. Their central institute was in the capital. When I first began attending their school in Sivas, my family did not have to pay any tuition fees. Of course, the fact that these priests were willing to educate the locals for free encouraged the locals to wonder as to the reason why they acted so generously. The accepted view was that like the American Protestant missionaries who had their own school in town, the Jesuits' primary aim had been to convert the local Muslims to Catholicism, and that after failing to make any inroads with them, they had changed tactics and now intended to convert the local Apostolic Armenians.

The Jesuit school, called the College Des Quarante Martyrs (The Institute of the Forty Martyrs), had seven grade levels. On a daily basis, we had one hour of French classes, one hour of Turkish, and one hour of Armenian, in addition to the other classes. The school was located at the confluence of two streams that were two arms of the River Halys and had a neat chapel where the pupils gathered every morning and attended Mass, which would last about half an hour. We also had to attend Sunday Mass. Only on Christmas and Easter did we have a chance to visit our own Armenian Apostolic Church. After some time, I even became an altar boy and learned the Mass in Latin. We altar boys were called Enfants Jesuses (Young Jesuses). At a later date, I also joined the choir, which was called Marie ou Conference. I also recited French poems and took part in plays in French, Armenian, and Turkish.

The school quickly gained popularity, and in 1908, it was enlarged with the purchase of lands that surrounded its original campus. Additionally, a new, modern, four-story stone building was built in the courtyard. Its first floor was composed of a kitchen, a visiting room, and a couple of other rooms. The second floor included a comfortable living room, offices, and a small chapel. The two uppermost floors were reserved as bedrooms for the priests and the teachers.

They later built a modern gymnasium, and, at great personal expense to Pere De Lavernette, the schoolmaster, a new chapel outside, four times bigger than the original chapel, with an alcove for the organ and a special platform for the choir. At this point, the old building was entirely converted into a school, and, unfortunately, to defray some of the costs of the renovations, a tuition fee was established. At this point, my mother was not able to pay the fee, so I decided to take a sabbatical from my studies and work for a while in order to save the necessary money. When my brothers heard of this, they opposed the idea. Hovhanness immediately told me to go back to school, saying he would pay the tuition fee. My brother Kaloust pledged to pay for the costs of my meals. For a while, things went well, but my tuition wasn't paid for the fourth month of the year. My brother Hovhanness did not seem to care at this point, so I decided to take some time off from my studies and began working. However, when he heard of my decision, Pere De Lavernette, a Jesuit Priest from Marzevon, called me into his office at 9:00 a.m. the next morning. He told me that the previous headmaster, Pere Briar, had told him how bright of a student I was, and that it was a shame for someone like me to leave school, even if temporarily. He told me that he, himself, was willing to pay for the costs of my tuition, textbooks, and writing implements, as long as my family was willing to pay for a month and a half of costs. My brother Kaloust agreed to make this payment, and thus, I was able to return to class. I kissed his hand in gratitude before I left the office.

However, this didn't mean that I didn't have to work. I was already helping my mother, and now, despite the fact that I was attending school, I took jobs to support her and the family. Despite this, my grades in school did not suffer. For some time, I took a job at my brother Kaloust's coffee and smoke shop. People gathered there to smoke cigars, and I pleasantly surprised Kaloust by learning very quickly how to roll cigars for his customers. Soon after that, Kaloust left for America, and I was faced with the burden of being the family's main breadwinner.

When Kaloust left, I took a job with a local photographer, named Dikran Zopapourian, and learned the trade within a month and a half. Sometime later, a Turkish officer, Ahmet Bey, who was in charge of a platoon of about 100 soldiers stationed in the city, asked me to teach him French on Sundays. I taught him vocabulary, grammar, and conversational French. My pay was 30 *Kurus*[1] per month. He also had two children, a son and a daughter. His daughter would often listen to the lessons, trying to learn French. She was a precocious girl—she had learned some Armenian words from the Armenian washer women, and she often teased me by telling me that she liked me in Armenian and then pretending that she didn't know what the words she used meant. These lessons would have continued for a while if the officer's brother-in-law, a man named Ismail, had not caught a contagious disease. Ahmet Bey decided to suspend the lessons for a while, at least until his brother-in-law recovered, which took quite a while. I never did return to their home.

Later, since I had learned how to draw, I also learned bookmaking. I got a job with a Turkish bookmaker in town and worked there for a while, also sometimes making books for myself. Another job I had was on the railroad—my friend Levon was able to find me a job on the line between Sivas and Samsun. The engineers' helper, Octave Gilbert, agreed to give me a job because I could speak both French and Turkish and could help the French staff members understand their Turkish customers. Finally, I worked for a local French family, Madam Rose's family. I did their shopping and ran errands, making about 30 Mejids[2] a month. They liked me, and they offered me a permanent job with them, but I refused, deciding instead to focus on my education.

Around this time, probably in 1913, I was also offered another opportunity that could have completely changed my life. My brother Dikran, who, by that point, lived in the United States, wrote to me saying that he would pay for my travel expenses from Marseilles to the New World if I were to accompany his wife on the journey. I still would have to pay for my passage from Sivas to Istanbul and from the capital to Marseilles. Although his wife was anxious to go on the journey, my mother was opposed to the idea of me going on the voyage. Besides, I only had a year and a half left before I graduated from school, and I wanted to complete my studies.

§§§

Our school was run differently from the other schools in Sivas. The city's Armenian and American schools were out on Saturdays, while our school had a full day on Saturdays and a half day on Thursdays. Our classroom was divided into two sections on a weekly basis. Every week, the best two students were announced, who in their turn divided the class into two groups. At the end of the next week, the grades of the two groups were compared and two students again chosen to head the groups.

The school's administration included Pere (Father) D'Antoine, who was the general administrator of the Jesuit schools and was based in Istanbul, the Ottoman capital. Our school's headmaster and general director was Pere De Lavernette, with whom I would later develop a close friendship. The teachers included Pere Daddon, who taught catechism and theology; Pere Sabatier, who taught botany and also conducted the school's brass band; Pere D'Arcier, who taught French; Pere Michel, who taught mathematics; Pere Pascal, who taught philosophy; Hovhanness Hermuzian, who taught Armenian to the upper classes; Khachadour Fenerjian, who taught French to fourth graders; Kaloust Ankaghian, who taught Armenian to fifth graders; Mikayel Terjanian, who taught French to first graders; and Mkrditch Kantarian. The assistant to the headmaster was an Armenian named Avedis Semerdjian, and two other Armenians, Senekerim Bachioghian and Krikor Kdikian, were members of the general staff. Other teachers included Senekerim Baliozian, Harutyun Zaratzian, and Vahe Jinbashian.

The schoolmaster, Pere De Lavernette, was the son of a noble family back in his native France. Ever since he had succeeded Pere Briar to become the schoolmaster, he had made very extensive improvements to the College. First he had enlarged the grounds by purchasing large, adjacent parcels of land. He had built a new, large auditorium that featured a stage. He had renovated the main chapel. He had built the new four-story stone building to house our teachers, complete with a reception room, kitchen, and dining room, and adorned with a small chapel with a bell tower. This building was a gem among the many other famous buildings of Sivas. The whole institution sat on a large plain between two streams. These beautiful buildings, some built using the schoolmaster's personal funds, would later be expropriated and desecrated.

The institution was mostly left unmolested when it was first established. It was divided into three separate levels—an elementary school, a middle school—the *cours moyen*—and the *cours superieur* (upper-level courses). Three years of classes comprised each level. For the upper class courses, students had to pay a fee after the expansion of the school. We, the students of the *cours superieur*, stood out thanks to our dark blue uniforms with brass buttons. In the entire school, there was only one Turkish student, Salim *Effendi*, the son of Avni Pasha, the commander of the Army division stationed in Sivas, the twenty-seventh Division of the Ottoman Army.

I remember our Armenian teacher with particular fondness. Mr. Hermuzian was a tireless educator, and thanks to his efforts, we became familiar with the greatest of Armenian writers of the time, including Siamanto and Daniel Varoujan. In fact, to compete with the magazine *Nishdag*, which was published by the Aramian Armenian School, we started our own literary journal called *Aghavni* (Pigeon). It was published once a month, and in it we tried to familiarize our readers with some of the contemporary Armenian literature, including much that was written by alumni of the school. We also wrote many articles that appeared in the journal. We wished to have more time dedicated to the study of the Armenian language and Armenian history, but only one hour a day was allotted to those subjects. However, thanks to the popular demand, and with the blessing and at the expense of the headmaster, Mr. Mihran Isberian, who was a teacher at the Aramian School and a renowned Armenian linguist, would visit twice a week and hold one-hour sessions, lecturing on Armenian literature. He was so moved by our dedication to his lectures that he often stayed for two hours instead of the one that he was paid for. We were enthralled by what he taught us. Alas, this arrangement did not last very long, only a few months.

I was fourteen years old when I joined the brass band of the school, and I stayed in the band for two years. I learned how to play the cornet, and like the other members of the band, I was given a special uniform to distinguish me from the other students. The band was split into two groups—those who knew how to read musical notes and those who didn't. At the end of that school year, we took a music test. I passed the test and was henceforth part of the group that knew how to read notations. I was awarded a silk tie to celebrate my success. The brass band performed four times a year for the local dignitaries. When the American missionaries established their Teachers' College in the city, the band was invited to play during the ceremonies.

The brass band of the Forty Martyrs School. Yervant Alexanian is at the forefront, seated on the ground, first from the left, holding his cornet.

The students in the highest grade had to take special exams each year, alongside all the prospective graduates of seven or eight other Jesuit schools in nearby cities. We were tested on all sorts of subjects and languages. There was also a writing competition, and all essays were sent to a central location (Istanbul) where they were ranked. I remember that in 1912, the topic for the French essay competition was "a description of a fire." The Marzavan Jesuit school came first, and Sivas ranked fourth. The individual winner was one Y. Aliksanian from our school. On this occasion, the entire school was awarded a half-day holiday. In the same year, Amira Dirhanian from Sivas won the Armenian-language writing competition. The topic had been a description of one of the year's four seasons, and Amira had described spring. Every year I would win four to five prizes in various areas.

§§§

When it came to sports and outdoor activities, the city's Armenian school, the Aramian School was the first to organize a boy scouting movement. They named their scouting club *Bertevagoump* and entrusted its leadership to Armenak Dumanian. A year later, our school, too, organized a scouting group that was called *L'Avant Garde* or the Forward Guard. In 1914, the Turkish school in Sivas, Sultanieh, organized its own scouting troupe and named it Izji.

These three troupes were distinguished by their unique uniforms. Members of *Bartevagoump* wore white shirts, short pants, and long socks. The Izjis wore black shirts, short pants, and always carried six-foot staffs that were at least two fingers thick. This weapon made the message they wanted to relay to others crystal clear. The French *Avant Garde* wore long-sleeved, striped, red shirts, neckerchiefs of the same material and color, knee socks of dark yellow, and yellow belts.

These troupes breathed new life into the life of Sivas. There were horse races and wrestling matches. Most of these usually ended in brawls, especially when an Armenian won the event. Among the Armenian, Simon Pehlijian was well known as the best fighter.

These wrestling and horse race events were organized in town once a year. Armenian athletes often gained notoriety when they won these contests. They were usually trained by Armenak Dumanian himself.

The 1913, the pan-Sivas "Olympic" games were a great event for all the scouting troupes. The *Bertevagoump* took the most medals, gaining the admiration of all. During the medal ceremonies, all Armenian athletes stood and sang the Turkish anthem when the flag was raised,

A picture of scouts sent to Yervant Alexanian in 1926, probably a good representation of what scouts wore at the time. The scout on the left is Antranig Habeshian, Yervant Alexanian's paternal cousin.

demonstrating again how loyal they actually were to the country in which they lived.

It's important to remember that before the deportations, we Armenians were very much involved not only with athletic competitions or scouting movements but also with the celebrations in Sivas. It always gave me great joy to participate in the performances of these different bands during the holidays and to hear them play their music so proudly outside of the government building. Before 1914, Armenians were very much part of the fabric of Sivas, and nobody would have believed that they could be annihilated so quickly, so unceremoniously. Nobody would anticipate what was to befall us, even those who had survived the many pogroms and massacres, such as the Hamidian massacres, that preceded the Genocide of 1915.

§§§

I remember much from my days in school. A singular fact was that ninety-five percent of the students in both the boys' and girls' schools were non-Catholic. Yet, the regulations were strict—every morning, we were to attend Mass before class. It usually lasted about twenty minutes and was always performed in Latin. Even on Sundays, at noon, we were all made to attend Mass, which was also attended by the French council and his family, in addition to some other French men, their wives, and their children. At the time, a group of French engineers was supervising a large project that was attempting to extend the water piping network to homes. It had been a government contract and had been awarded to the French firm these engineers represented. These were the Frenchmen and their families who attended Mass with us.

The school never advocated rebellion against the government or any form of anti-Islamic ideology. Allow me to demonstrate by retelling a story that I remember as if it happened yesterday. I remember, it was the first day of the Muslim holidays, a day that we children always looked forward to. Holidays were always a cause for excitement, whether Christmas and New Year, or the Turkish holidays, during which the archways in the center of the city were decorated with streamers and with small lanterns. This particular celebration took place in 1914, before the declaration of the Great War, and in that year, the start of the Muslim holidays coincided with the anniversary of the reformation of the Ottoman Constitution of 1908. On that day, all of the schools were closed, and the students of the local Turkish schools, the American school, the French school, and the Aramian Armenian School gathered in the square outside of the government building, ready to partake in the day's festivities. We were there before noon. At the designated time, the day's guests, mostly the town's dignitaries, political and religious leaders, and community leaders, alongside the representatives of local political parties, the provincial governor, and the police, arrived and took their designated seats. Also present was the local Turkish scouting troupe, dozens of policemen to ensure order, and a large portion of the town's population. The event was opened by a performance of the military band. The American school's band also played wonderfully, followed by the French school's brass band. I was among the members of this brass band. I played the cornet. These performances were followed by speeches on the part of the day's guests and other dignitaries. They all unanimously praised the 1908 Ottoman Constitution, outlining how much it had helped both the country's Turks and the country's minorities. After the formal speeches, the master of ceremonies suggested that Murad, too, make a speech. He was a student at our school and one of the most intelligent. He had sat the whole time among the other guests, his shoulders wide, his glance imperturbable, as if trying to upstage the others around him. He was not particularly fluent in Turkish, as his speech demonstrated, but he did not shirk from the task, and stepping forward, began: "Thank you all. We are gathered here today to celebrate the anniversary of the reformed Ottoman constitution, which rests on four pillars—the pillars of freedom, equality, brotherhood, and justice. May God bless those who struggle to keep these four pillars standing!"

I tell this story not as a simple recollection, but as evidence of the loyalty of Armenian subjects to their Ottoman masters, as well as evidence that the French Jesuits were by no means inspiring their students to rebel. Despite the Turks' assertions, Armenian and Christian schools, organizations, and groups in Sivas were not preaching separatism or advocating revolution. They were, in fact, doing their best to preach loyalty to the government and to raise a generation that remained loyal to the Ottoman court.

I remember how earlier in 1914, at the end of June, the College's year-end graduation ceremony was held in the newly built auditorium. This was before the start of the war, when things were still relatively calm and peaceful. The auditorium was packed with parents and invited dignitaries. The ceremony began with the singing of the *Marseillaise*,[3] followed by the Ottoman anthem, both sung by a school's choir. One of the events of the night featured Salim *Effendi*, the son of Avni Pasha, our only Turkish student, reciting a poem written by his proud father titled "A Salute to the Turkish Flag (*Sama Salam, Osmanli Bayragi*)." When the yearly prizes were being given out, Mr. Semerdjian called my name as the recipient of the prize of excellence. I had been chosen through a secret ballot of the faculty. The headmaster, beaming proudly, sifted through a large stack of prizes and picked a gilded trophy, which he handed to Governor Mouammer, who in turn handed it to me. But first, he placed a crown upon my head. The prize itself was a large Turkish history book bound in red leather and embossed with golden lettering. I was extremely embarrassed by the attention, and after gingerly taking the prize from the governor, I nodded my head in appreciation, then limped back to my seat.

My friend Shushan, too, was in the crowd, since she was a student at the school of the French St. Joseph nuns, a Catholic school for girls attached to ours. I noticed her in the crowd, and I remember smiling at her and how she smiled back.

I did not know that this would be the first and last time that the auditorium would be used. Four months later, by the order of the same governor who had handed me my prize, it would be taken over.

It's important to remember that Avni Pasha, whose son attended our school, would later, during the massacres, try to intervene and save at least a few Armenian lives. He suggested that a list be made and that families of Armenian soldiers serving in the army be spared deportation. If this recommendation had been accepted, my family would have been saved. Unfortunately, the request was denied by Governor Mouammer, and Avni Pasha, who, by his action, had proven himself too soft toward the Armenians was quickly replaced by a younger and much more brutal colonel named Pertev Bey.

§§§

In September 1914 began our new school year at the College Des Quarante Martyrs, which, as had already been mentioned, was founded and administered by French priests who belonged to the Jesuit Order. This was to be my last year at the institution. There were five of us who were on course to graduate—Vahan Yakoubian, Garabed Injeian, Khersantos Kalayjoglu (he used to sign his name Kalajian), Simon Mozian, and I. I was slated to graduate at the top of my class.

By that point, the large majority of Armenian families in Sivas had elected to send their children to the Quarante Martyrs School. In fact, for us pupils, being students of this school inspired us with pride. We knew we were receiving the best education we could receive in a city like Sivas.

Even though in July of that year World War I had broken out, and Turkey had immediately declared war on the side of Germany, life was regaining a sense of normalcy. The general belief was that the war would last no more than five or six months, at the most.[4] I remember how we, the pupils, were encouraged to contribute to the national war effort with cash and linen that was to be sent to the front. I also remember that when the war first started, despite the sanguine impression that the government wanted to impart, the country was clearly unprepared for the conflict. There was a dearth of space to accommodate all the soldiers who were traveling through Sivas, and they had to be quartered in citizens' homes. From the very beginning of the war, there was a shortage of food and medicine. Many of the soldiers hadn't been issued official uniforms and wore animal skins instead to differentiate themselves from civilians.

For us, things took a turn for the worst on the fateful morning of November 5, 1914, right after the third-month exams. Pere De Lavernette, the schoolmaster, walked into our classroom, accompanied by his assistant, Mr. Avedis Semerdjian. He looked utterly dejected. His voice shaking, he began speaking: "Yesterday, Governor Mouammer summoned me to his office and gave me the order to immediately close this institution. We priests have been given one week to leave the country and return to France." He added that the same order was also to apply to the girls' school that the French Jesuit nuns ran, which was located in the building adjacent to ours. Clearly, the aim of the order was not just to shut down the schools but to eliminate the presence of the Jesuits on Turkish soil. The school administration had been told that all of the school's possessions could be stored in the four attic rooms of the four-story stone building. The government had pledged to seal the four doors, and the Governor had given his personal word of honor that nothing would be touched until the priests returned. He had claimed that not even a pin would be missing when the priests returned, whenever they returned. The schoolmaster could barely finish speaking. He was in tears, and he rushed out of the classroom, only to have to go and relay the same message to the other classes. Mr. Semerdjian, staying behind, told us to gather our books and go home, as the school was, in effect, closed.

Alas, events belied the good Father's words. Before he and his compatriots had even reached the port of Samsun, where they were to board the ship that was to take them back to France, the seals of the four locks were broken. The contents of the attic rooms were carried to the nearby Sultanieh Turkish school, by the school's own pupils. I even saw my own cornet, which I had played with such gusto in the school brass band, being carried away by a young Turkish boy.

About three weeks later, the same governor, Mouammer, and the police commissioner, Kelash Bey, were at the head of a bloodthirsty mob that gathered around the school's stone building. The two officials leading the crowd were accompanied by a man who was called Gomali *Hoja*, because he always carried a dagger hanging from his belt. First, the crowd, its passions flared, violently removed the cross that sat atop the small chapel and replaced it with a crescent. This was done in some sort of ceremonial fashion. As to the main church, they destroyed the Altar, the beautiful statues, the stained-glass paintings, and the pews. This house of worship was converted into a house of convalescence for Turkish soldiers wounded on the front. Within a short time, the church looked like a dirty stable.

Allow me to add that this *Hoja*, who was an imam at the local mosque, had, every Friday since the start of the war, used his pulpit to instigate hatred against all non-Muslims, especially against Armenians.

§§§

A few months after the closure of the school, some of the Armenian teachers who had been left behind attempted to resurrect the school, teaching out of rooms in the residents of a man called *Shekerdji* Kaloust. Very quickly, they were ordered to desist by the authorities.

Notes

1. Ottoman currency. 100 Kurus = One Mejid or Lira (Pound).
2. Equivalent to the Ottoman Lira (Pound).
3. The French national anthem.
4. An interesting footnote of history—in almost all warring states during World War I, the general belief was that the hostilities would not last more than a few months. Naturally, all thought they would be the victors.

3

Life in Sivas before Deportations

As I got a bit older, and especially after the closure of my school, I began truly noticing the discrimination and prejudice Armenians were subjected to. After the closure of my school, I could not remain idle, and besides, as the Turkish economy deteriorated, I had to help the family. So, I was employed at the store of Giragos Hajinlian, who made a good living selling cutlery, crockery, household items, and other trinkets out of his store. I had worked for him part-time occasionally during my school years, and when he offered me a full-time position, I accepted it gladly. My pay was 4 *Mejid* per month. I began working at his store on November 10, 1914. I only got to work there for six months before the deportations began.

One day, while I was busy helping a customer at the store, I noticed a young man in uniform loitering outside. He seemed to be carefully studying the various items we had on display at the store-front, particularly the watch chains. Suddenly, he burst through the door, and without

Alexanian and his mother Hunazant, in 1910.

37

waiting in line, came up to the counter and banged his fist against it. He demanded to see a watch chain he had seen in the window. I was taken aback. Unable to refuse him, and doing my best to keep my composure, I obliged. When I placed the chain on the counter, he took it up, and examined it closely for a few minutes. He then announced that he had seen a few more chains in the window that he may be interested in. I walked over to the display window with him again and took the ones he pointed out back to the counter. He took his time now, trying each chain on his wrist, completely oblivious to the consternation of the other customers who, after all, could do nothing about the situation. He ordered me to bring over the rest of the chains, and I complied, thinking to myself that I had just met the most selfish man in the world. He kept trying the chains out, then tossing them pell-mell all over the counter. After a while, I finally dared open my mouth: "Sir, have you found a chain that you like?"

"What's your rush, you son of a dog?" he roared, and his hand hovered ominously above the pistol at his hip, "don't you forget, you're nothing but a *geyavour*, and you're speaking to a Muslim! I could finish you off right now and nobody would give a damn!"

Then, he glanced at the people in the store, who had been patiently waiting for service and now looked terrified. He seemed to hesitate, then he looked into my eyes and whispered: "You just wait a few days, and see what happens . . . Some of our boys will be going to Tokat[1] to deal with your people there . . . They'll be back in a day or two, then it'll be your turn . . . " and he quickly turned and walked out of the store, while I and the store's astonished patrons exchanged incredulous looks.

Barely an hour later, while I was in the store, by myself, still mulling over the terrorizing threat I had received, a Turkish army officer, accompanied by seven or eight infantrymen, burst in through the door. Acting in an insultingly peremptory manner, the officer announced that the army at the front, fighting under the banner of Sultan, was in great need of a large amount of cutlery and crockery.

"Show me where you keep your stocks, right away!" he roared. This whole time, his men were picking various items off our shelves with careless abandon.

The officer didn't even give me the time to respond. Before I could process his request, he turned to his men and ordered them to take the items they had piled on the counter outside. He then glanced around the room, and noticing some more plates behind the counter, ordered one of his men to take those, and yet another man was ordered to take the large trays. Soon, it dawned on me that they were basically robbing us blind, carrying whatever they could out of the place. I tried in vain to ask for explanations, hoping that I would at least stall them long enough for my employer to return and see them there, saving me the task of explaining everything to him later. The only response I could get from the officer was that the Ottoman government would reimburse us for our losses. He sneered and added "soon you'll see!" menacingly. I begged him to give me official paperwork confirming his promise, imploring him to consider my situation with my employer, who would surely want to see official papers. The officer considered the matter for a few moments and then ordered me to get some paper. On it, he wrote "Aldi" in Turkish, meaning requisition, and gave the paper back to me: "Give this to your employer!" he said, and turned away. I and the store were basically mugged in clear daylight.

§§§

As the war prolonged beyond expectation, we kept seeing more and more soldiers passing through the city, heading for the Russian front. The news that leaked out was not encouraging for the Ottoman army. Too many wounded soldiers were brought back home for rehabilitation. Meanwhile, some terrible news was received by Mr. Giragos from his hometown of Kayseri. His older brother Krikor Hajinlian had been beaten up by the local authorities. He and other Armenians who had been assaulted had been injured so badly that they had been sent back home, bleeding, in a horse-driven cart. Right around the same time, Mr. Asadour Ehmalian from Gurmerak, one of our best customers, was in Sivas to shop. Ehmalian was the scion of a very wealthy family in his hometown, where he owned a very large variety store. All we knew was that he had been arrested in Sivas and sent to jail. Mr. Hajinlian gave me the task of taking food to him, as we all knew they would barely give him any in jail. When I saw him, he was shackled in very heavy chains. He could hardly walk. This was a man who had committed no crime. He was happy to see me and was in good spirits. He did not know why he had been arrested nor did he know why he was being held in such conditions. He was sure that he would be free in a few days as there was no reason for detaining him. Instead, without a trail, they sentenced him to death. While visiting him in jail, I also saw eight to ten Russian prisoners of war. One of them was Armenian, and he later escaped the jail at night.

When I went back to the store, Mr. Hajinlian and some other friends were discussing the situation. I told them what I had seen that morning.

§§§

Let nobody think that just because the situation was getting worse and worse for Armenians, money and influence had lost their power. This is perfectly illustrated in the story of Dr. Hagop Jessourian. This doctor was a young man in his late twenties. He, like many others, was drafted into the Turkish Army and reached the rank of captain. He was young, slim, and had a pointy beard. He looked quite handsome in his military garb. One day he came with his brother Sebouh. They had a lengthy, private conversation with Mr. Giragos. As the two brothers left, I heard Sebouh saying—"Giragos, see what you can do, money is no object. As you see, my brother is absolutely innocent. The whole thing is fabricated. It is a false accusation by his colleagues."

The next thing we knew was that Dr. Jessourian had been arrested, was in prison, and was to be dragged before a military tribunal—a sham trial, undoubtedly. So serious was the charge that he faced that there was a real possibility he would be sentenced to death by firing squad. No wonder Mr. Giragos was calling up his connections within the court. A few days later, he walked into the store with an elderly army captain, who was one of the members of the said tribunal. The captain picked out a few things to buy, then asked, "How much do I owe?"

"Don't you worry about it, we'll talk about it on Saturday at my house!" replied Mr. Giragos.

And in fact, next thing I knew, Mr. Giragos had arranged for a party to be hosted on the following Saturday evening, to which, besides the old captain, three other high-ranking officers were invited. He asked me to serve at the party, and he hired three known musicians to provide entertainment. When I showed up on Saturday evening, I was surprised—there were many more officers there than I had expected, and they ranked higher than I had expected. The atmosphere was jovial, and Mr. Giragos repeatedly borrowed the officers' swords to dance.

His efforts paid off—Dr. Hagop's trial was repeatedly postponed. Occasionally, the doctor's brother Sebouh would travel from Azzizieh, a town quite far from Sivas, where he and his family were known as being one of the wealthiest in the area, and would return with money to pay Mr. Giragos to cover the costs of the parties and the gifts. Sebouh always said that money was no object and that Mr. Giragos shouldn't be stingy, as long as Dr. Jessourian was eventually released. Finally, two months after this charade, the trial was held. Dr. Jessourian was acquitted of all charges, citing lack of evidence.

§§§

One day, I was going from store to store running errands, when I saw a large crowd of Turks attacking a young, strapping Armenian man. The young man was courageously trying to parry the punches thrown at him, while at the same time trying to make his escape. He was up against huge odds, despite his apparent physical prowess.

The crowd reached the corner of the street on which my brother's store was located. I was afraid the mob would get out of control. Fortunately for us, just at that moment, a Turkish man, perhaps around the age of thirty, rushed toward the crowd, wishing to take his fill of the violence. He swung at the Armenian youth, who, however, was much quicker, and avoiding the strike, counterattacked the Turk and splayed him onto the ground. In the confusion that ensued, Khorsa *Emmi*,[2] a local Turk who owned a textile shop right around the corner, was able to whisk the Armenian youth into his shop. He then came outside and locked the door of his shop from the outside. He addressed the crowd, telling them to be ashamed of their behavior, and reprimanding them for being afraid of a *geyavour*. Somehow, he was able to disperse the mob. This is how most clashes between Armenians and Turks ended in Sivas—either with the intervention of respected, elderly patriarchs or with the intervention of the police. Of course, sometimes, both of these parties turned a blind eye when the victims of violence were Armenians. So, whenever Turks and Armenians were in conflict, the Turks simply resorted to violence, fully aware that at that point, they would be given free hand to strong-arm the Armenians. Whenever it came to blows, they would simply yell out—*Immet Musulman Yokme!*, or, "Will nobody help a Muslim!", and these words would conjure a mob out of nowhere. Of course, any Armenians who fought back would be marked men and wouldn't be able to walk about freely in town. When young Armenian men physically resisted the Turks, their parents would swallow the bitter pill and send them overseas or to other parts of the country, where these embittered youth would have to rebuild their lives. Families were broken up over trivial disputes in markets and on the streets.

§§§

I knew that the situation in the city was untenable, and that I, too, would soon fall victim to a twist of fate. By this point, Turks were openly harassing Armenians in the city. One teenage boy even died after he jumped into the river, after being harried by Turkish teenagers with swords. None of them were punished. The Turks began taking prisoners a few days before June 3, 1915. Then, for a few days, they told Armenians that they could open their stores and wouldn't be harried, but this was a ruse, and many were still arrested and thrown into jail.

On that day, my uncle Misak Parseghian and my cousin Tateos (Thaddeus) were among those who were arrested. At first, we were told that they would be released within a few days. Unfortunately, this was proven to be a false promise—they were kept in jail for some time, deprived of food and of basic necessities. They were kept under lock and key until the deportations, at which time they were taken outside the city and executed. Many of the men who were jailed with them had gone insane by this time.

It was also around this time when I personally witnessed an act of sheer barbarity. Father Sahak was the priest of the Armenian Church in Erzincan,[3] and he happened to be in Sivas. One morning, I saw his chariot driving down the road. I was at the store and saw him through the window panes. Later that night, I saw the same chariot returning. The priest wasn't in it. Instead, the coach was occupied by Hussein, the son of Kertooki, a local Turk. He had killed the priest. His only injury was a light wound on his foot.

Another prominent Armenian from the city, Baruyr Boghossian, who worked as an accountant, was invited to the house of a high-ranking Turkish official from the city and was never seen again.

Also, the Damlamian Brothers, Yerserjian and Garjian, prominent rug makers who lived in the city, were also arrested.

Around this time, more of my family members were detained. One of my brothers was arrested, because *gendarmes*[4] had asked him to tell them where I was. Having not found me at Hajinlian's store, the policemen detained my brother. Their aim was to arrest me, because I had to enlist in the army. They eventually let him go, telling him to bring me to them, and slapped him across the face a couple of times for good measure.

After being let go, my brother found me and immediately took me to the police station. Thankfully, hearing of what had happened, Mr. Giragos and some other family friends came to the police station to get me out. The *gendarmes* had us all lined up in a room and made us pledge loyalty to the Sultan—"Long Live the Sultan!" At that point, *Asbonjou* Oghlu, one of the *gendarmes*, called out my name and freed me. Mr. Hajinlian had saved me from prison and probably from being dragooned into the army. But the signal was clear—I could be arrested and taken into the army at any time. The next day, when I went to work, I told Mr. Hajinlian that I would henceforth accept no wages from him, for as long as I worked for him.

§§§

Around this time, the town's priest announced in church that the government had decided to move the town's Armenian population elsewhere, where a new Armenian town was going to be built, specially for them. The following Sunday, the entire Armenian community of Sivas was at Church, overflowing the knaves and spilling into the courtyard. There was not an inch to spare. The prelate, Father Torkom Kalemkerian, reiterated the order of the government, confirming that no reprieve had been granted by officials.

The last words of his sermon are branded into the memory of most Sivas Armenians who survived the subsequent events—"My dear compatriots, the ship of the Armenian people is stuck in stormy waters, and is in clear and present danger of capsizing. The port is so close, but the captain can't do anything to get us to that safe haven. He struggles with the till, his sailors struggle with the sails, but there's not even a distant glimmer of hope. The government's decision is irrevocable. They won't yield. They won't even allow me to accompany you, my flock. I will be kept here. The government has been told that some people have stashed weapons in this Church. I'm to stay here while they tear it down and look for them. Of course, I don't have to remind you that most of us revere our Church so much that we don't even dare enter it shod."

The Patriarch, was in fact, kept in Sivas after most Armenians were deported. He was present to witness the city's churches being taken apart and robbed.

When he came to the end of his sermon, he tried to inspire the people with courage, telling us we should be strong when faced with pain and suffering. He blessed us all, and with a quivering voice, he sang the closing hymns of the service.

The ceremony ended with heartfelt prayers and blessings. The people went home with tears streaming from their eyes, preparing themselves for the worst. The first neighborhood from Sivas to be deported was the Bezia neighborhood, which was deported on June 22, 1915.

It is worth mentioning here that Apostolic Armenians were not the only ones who suffered. Talaat Pasha[5] had promised that Catholic and Protestant Armenians would be spared the deportations, no doubt because he wanted to ingratiate himself with the western powers. However, the Catholic inhabitants of the village of Perkenik, near Sivas, were also deported, as were Protestant Armenians.

Also, at around the same time, the population of the Armenian town of Tavra near Sivas, who were descendent of master flour mill operators, were forced into Islam and dispersed around the Empire, thus ensuring that the flour mills of the Turkish towns were kept in good order.

§§§

On June 7, 1915, I heard that the *gendarmes* were looking for me again. They had gone to my brother's house again. Getting this news, I decided to write a letter to Ahmet *Effendi*, whom I had taught French some time ago. In the letter, I asked him for help. My mother delivered the letter for me, but he responded by saying he could not help. I was forsaken and waited for the next twist of fate that would befall me.

It was June 5, 1915. I was on my way to Mr. Hajinlian's store, for my daily shift at work. First, I saw an Armenian woman on the road, and she told me that the Turks were hanging Armenian men. I didn't consider it to be breaking news, since that had been happening quite often, so I kept walking. But before reaching the end of our block, I saw our friend Avedis Samdjian returning home from the city center. His face was pale with fear. He prevented me from going further and told me to stay home. He told me that the *gendarmes* were taking Armenians, suspected of dodging the general mobilization order, to the police station. Policemen, working in pairs, were falling upon Armenian men they found and taking them away. Shopkeepers who had just opened their businesses had to abandon everything and follow the police. Others were detained before even getting to work. None of them had any idea why they were being taken away. In this way, in one single morning, the great majority of the Armenian adult male population of the city disappeared, filling the city jail. Many of them were later decapitated. I replied by saying that I was not yet old enough to be drafted, so I didn't have anything to worry about. He said it didn't matter—young or old, they were taking every Armenian. "Just stay home!" he implored. I followed his advice. This was a Friday morning. Unfortunately, the future would prove that even his heartfelt advice was futile—those who didn't go to work that day, and weren't arrested, were not spared the future horrors that befell all Armenians in the Ottoman Empire. They were deported alongside their families. Regardless, after hearing what he had to say, I went back home and cloistered myself inside.

The barracks of the twenty-seventh Division of the Ottoman Army were located near Sivas; all of the young men from the city, from its suburbs, and from nearby villages who were to enlist were to be sent to those barracks to register and receive their commissions. The building used to belong to an Armenian named Poutakian, which had been expropriated by the government. The actual enlistment center was a large, comfortable house at the end of the Virgin Mary Street that had been expropriated from local Armenians. As soon as the mobilization orders had been issued, this enlistment center had become the focus of an extraordinary amount of traffic. The city was suddenly buzzing with activity, especially the market district. On a daily basis, hundreds, if not thousands of fresh conscripts and half-trained troops, sometimes organized into squadrons, either loitered around or marched through the streets. Sometimes, we even saw squads heading to the front lines. The numbers swelled to such an extent that the government could not procure them all with proper uniforms, and we saw many men heading into battle dressed *in mufti*. Knowing they would not be supplied properly, many of them carried bags or satchels full of food they had purchased with their own funds. They wore their thick peasants' mantles on their backs, in preparation for the frosts of the coming winter. They usually walked in columns of four men abreast, led by their officers.

Sivas, which had always been more of a backwater, suddenly became a center of military activity and planning thanks to its proximity to the front. Naturally, this had a huge stimulating effect on the economy. Impromptu eateries, cobblers, and shops appeared out of nowhere. The market district buzzed with activity at all hours of the day.

Regardless, I could enjoy none of this feverish activity in the city, as I had to stay at home, in hiding, for the following three days. During this time, Nazeli, my sister-in-law, who was also an expert seamstress, was my daily companion. I was so bored that I soon became interested in the sewing machine that she kept in the house. In a strange twist of serendipity, during my incarceration, she taught me the basics of sewing, which would literally save my life later. She had been a renowned seamstress in town, trusted even by the local troops.

Yervant's brother Kaloust, who would later pay for him to migrate to the United States, and sister-in-law Nazeli, who taught him how to sew, and perished in the Genocide.

Later, when I was conscripted into the army as a tailor thanks to Nazeli's efforts to teach me sewing, I used some of the money I had made working at Hajinlian's store to buy Nazeli a spindle and a bookshelf.

That Sunday afternoon, two *gendarmes* came knocking at our door asking for me. They had their swords unsheathed and a piece of paper in their hands, undoubtedly containing the order to detain me. Nazeli and my cousin Yughaper told them that I was not at home, that I had gone to church. They did not believe them.

Meanwhile, Nazeli was able to slip away and pass me the news. She said that by order of the head of the recruiting office, *Kaimakam* [governor] Khalil Shukri Bey, I was being summoned before the recruiters. I had heard the name before. I told Nazeli to hold the *gendarmes* in conversation. I still wonder how in such a short amount of time, I was able to put my shoes on and run to the backyard, climb over two fences, and within five or six minutes present myself to Khalil Shukri Bey. He was a gentleman who used to come to our store a few times a week, after office hours, to chat with my boss and buy kitchen utensils. I used to deliver these utensils to his house. He was known as a fair man who helped Armenians. He had saved ten Armenians from being sent to the front. At the time, he lived right across the street from the Aramian School with his wife and two children. As a high-ranking officer, he was allowed to have two soldiers serving him at home. He had been given two Turkish soldiers by the Army, but he had decided to hire two Armenians soldiers instead, despite protests.

When Shukri Bey saw me he greeted me as a friend, saying that he had sent for me to be enlisted, but that perhaps he could do something for me if I knew a trade. I remembered how I had just learned how to sew. Therefore, my answer to Shukri Bey's question was yes, I knew how to sew. Immediately he called his secretary, Mehmet *Effendi*, into the room, gave him the order to enlist me into the army, and to transfer me the next day to the military workshop. I tried to get away from being drafted, reasoning that I was too young. I begged him to let me accompany my family on the march out of Sivas. But Shukri Bey cut me short: "My boy, your family will be moved away from Sivas soon, and if you leave with them, you will be picked up along the way anyway. I want you to stay here and serve your country." However, he still had to arrest me. I was taken to jail, but that same day, at 10:00 a.m., Mehmet *Effendi* came and freed me, to the shock of the Turks I was in jail with. He even asked me to buy him cherries as a reward for freeing me. I didn't have any money on me, but I promised I would buy them for him on the following day. On my way back home, I came face-to-face with Ahmet *Effendi* but said nothing to him. He had abandoned me in my time of need.

Mehmet *Effendi* told me to go home and return the following day without fail. This news shocked my mother, as we already knew we would be deported. There was no way to avoid the order. I now had two choices—I could either accompany my family on the road to the Syrian deserts, or I could remain in Sivas and serve under the banner of the country that was condemning them to death. I have never had to make such a difficult decision.

That evening, we all gathered at the home of my uncle Seropeh. There were many opinions expressed, much advice given to me, as to what I should do. I personally was not sure if Shukri Bey's advice was the one I should take. It could have been a ruse. One of the clients at Mr. Hajinlian's store, General Arzooman Bey, a former Kurdish pharmacist by profession, had told me to tear up my conscription form and go on to Syria with my family. He had said they had already created the towns in Syria where the Armenians would henceforth live. I thought he may have been lying, but I could not be sure. There was advice from everyone. I was still extremely undecided, but my mother had the final word: "Son, some of our family is in America. The rest of us are going to be forced to leave. God knows where we will end up. I've had ominous premonitions regarding our fate. It would be good if at least one of us stayed here. If something happens to us, at least you will still be alive. In any case, God will provide."

That is what I did. I stayed.

Shukri Bey would later retire in 1916. He was one of the few Turkish officials who seemed to genuinely care about the Armenians of the area. I later heard that Dertad Baynterian, who had been a secretary working for him, had tried to ask him to give me a menial job within his household, but the Bey knew he wouldn't receive permission to employ another Armenian, and he considered me being enlisted at the tailors' workshop as the next best thing.

§§§

By this time, the rights and freedoms of Armenians were being violated on a daily basis. Every morning we woke up facing new restrictions, new threats, and new discrimination. On a daily basis, about 50–100 Armenians would disappear from the city, most often from the jails, would be taken into the valleys surrounding the city, and would be murdered there. Fear had become the prevailing emotion of Armenians left in the city. Some people could not handle it and went insane, out of fear of the coming deportations. One of them was a man named Massis Odabashian. He could not tolerate the prospect of being butchered like cattle, and so he preferred to take his own life.

Notes

1. The city of Tokat, with a population of about 130,000, is the capital of Tokat Province near the Black Sea, in modern-day Central Turkey.
2. *Emmi* literally means uncle (a father's brother), but in context here likely refers to an avuncular local Turk.
3. City in modern-day Northeastern Turkey.
4. Armed police officers.
5. Mehmed Talaat Pasha was the Ottoman Minister of both Finance and the Interior after the Young Turk revolution, and part of the triumvirate that ruled the Empire during World War I. He is considered one of the main architects of the Armenian Genocide.

4

Deportations and Genocide

I was officially enlisted into the Ottoman Army on June 10, 1915, just weeks before my family was forcibly made to take the road of deportation. As they marched to their death, I began a new life in the workshop of the twenty-seventh *Kolordu* (Army Corps) of the Ottoman army. I was first sent to Dertad Baynterian's office, who confirmed that I knew how to sew. Then, I was sent to the twenty-seventh Division's Workshop.

The workshop was not built bespoke. It was the Aramian school building, which had hitherto been the only Armenian school in Sivas. The top floor was given to the cobblers, the large refectory to the tailors, and the classrooms adjacent to the refectory had been turned to bedrooms. Each "bedroom" housed at least thirty men. The basement floors contained the loot that had been stolen from Armenian merchants all over the city, including silk and leather used in the workshop. The top floor was given to the commander of the workshop, Ethim *Effendi*, and his assistants, among whom were three Armenians—Armenak Ayvazian, the son of a government official; Armenak Dumanian, who had been the leader of the *Bartevagoump* scouting troupe; and a man by the name of Krikor, who eventually became completely Turkified. The supervisor of the workshop was Lieutenant *Tokattsi* Hamdi Chavoush, a man renowned for his visceral hatred of Armenians.

At first, when I started working at the workshop, I was mocked by many of the Armenians already there for my lack of skill. I knew most of them. The majority of them were locals from Sivas or hailed from Tokat, Marzevan, or Amasia. I quickly realized that I would not be able to meet my daily quota. Thankfully, I quickly befriended the others, and they lent me a helping hand. They would put in extra time at work just to help me meet the requirements. Within two days, I could sew a complete pair of pants, and within five days, I'd learned to sew complete jackets, thanks to their patient mentoring. We worked with finger sewing machines that had been appropriated from an American company, and most of the textile we used had been confiscated from Armenian stores in the city. We were each expected to produce thirty-five to forty full uniforms per day. Whenever my colleagues helped me meet this quota, I would stand guard for them for a few hours every night whenever they wished to do something clandestine. The tailoring division for the workshop was directed by Haji *Kheghtzi*[1] Jeblents Mihran, an Armenian apostate who had converted to Islam. His Turkish name was *Ousda*[2] Ahmet. The head of my group of tailors was *Varbed* Nazar Odabashian, and his helpers included Yervant Khasierjian, Ohan *Varbed*, Melkon Chaderjian, and *Tokattsi*[3] Hagop. Naturally, all of the Armenian tailors who had owned shops in Sivas had been forced to close shop and work for the government in exchange for scraps of food. Most of their families were later deported and killed.

Lieutenant Ethem *Effendi*, the commander of the workshop, always did his best to exploit his Armenian troops as much as possible, to benefit from their unpaid labor to the maximum extent. *Ousda* Hagop, who had been a renowned furrier in Tokat, was ordered to make him a fur coat. He worked day and night, for weeks, to procure the best fur he could find and sewed it all together expertly. The result was amazing. *Ousda* Hagop was also ordered to make underwear for the Effendi, and he had made enough to last eight or ten years. Tailor Melkon Chaderjian and other master tailors like him made suits for Ethem Effendi, using some of the best textile that had been appropriated from the stores of local Armenian merchants, whose wares had been confiscated. He also made the shoemakers work for him. It was said that when the War ended, the Effendi would never again have to buy clothing or shoes.

Ethem Effendi was also particularly hated because his quarters were the rooms that had once housed the kindergarten of the Aramian School, where many of the children of these Armenian troops, now dead, had been educated.

We didn't get paid to work—all we received was one daily meal. Unfortunately, even this meal was barely sufficient to keep us alive. So, until the deportations, my mother would visit me at the workshop every day and bring me a meal to eat. The soldiers standing on guard always checked her parcels for bombs. One day, she wanted to speak to me so I left the barracks, but immediately, a Turkish officer grabbed me and pulled me back in. My mother tearfully begged him to allow us to speak for a few minutes. Eventually he relented, but insisted that the conversation should take place in Turkish, so that he could understand.

Until the last day before the deportations, my mother continued bringing me food on a daily basis.

One of the last times I saw her, she came to bring me the customary parcel, then tearfully told me that she and the rest of the family would be deported within five days. I couldn't eat that day, and I sobbed to myself. Ethem *Effendi*, seeing my state, and perhaps pitying me, told me that I would have an hour to visit with my family before they left. My mother, meanwhile, asked for permission to have me accompany the caravan on the march, but I was only given permission to accompany them on the first leg of the journey.

§§§

Of all my family members, including mother, uncles, aunts, cousins, etc., a total of fifty-one died. Of all my family members who lived in the Ottoman Empire at the time, only two cousins survived.

The deportations began a few days after the final announcement of Patriarch Kelemkerian in the *Asdvadzadzin* church and proceeded throughout the next few weeks. The official order of deportation was issued on June 15, 1915, and the Bezia neighborhood, the first to be deported, went on the death march on June 22, 1915. The Patriarch, politicians, and other influential Armenians had tried to intervene with the government and convince it to rescind its decision, but it had all been in vain. Everyone had to be uprooted, except for a few artisans and their families. These, however, had to accept Islam to be allowed to stay.

The people of Sivas and its environs, who had, for more than 600 years, tolerated the oppression and excesses of their brutal overlords, now had to pack up and leave their ancestral lands and homes, hoping against hope that the promise the government had made regarding them being given lands in Syria would be kept. They had to leave all they had worked for and go to lands they had never heard of. Worse yet, all of them had heard rumors that they could expect to be robbed, beaten, tortured, or perhaps even killed along the way.

The entire Armenian population of Sivas was deported within weeks. Every night, I saw caravans of deportees leave town, making their way to their deaths across the valleys that surrounded the city.

Some men were able to escape military service and were also not arrested while on business or in their shops. Some stayed home during those ominous days, and these took the road to deportation alongside their families. Included in this group were those who, putting their faith on the newly promulgated military regulations, had paid the

40 Turkish Pounds that allowed them to be exempt from obligatory military service. Among this latter group were my uncle's son-in-law, Zacharia Mankikian, from Arapkir, and my brother Hovhanness. They and their families were all deported. These men had put their trust in the Turkish government, hoping it would keep its word, but they were sadly not vindicated in their faith.

Whole households had to leave the only city they had known with all of their possessions crammed into a single chariot. Eventually came the turn of my neighborhood, on July 3, 1915. Like everyone else, the Armenians were told they would be taken to a peaceful, stable region, where they would be able to establish their own communities. They were told to leave their belongings behind that they would be sent after them. However, we all knew what was going on, so most Armenians sold most of their belongings at dirt cheap prices. My own family sold what it could, then left the rest of the furniture with the Kapikians, who were allowed to stay, and the rest of our items with various Turkish neighbors. I received permission from the barracks to accompany my family as far as the farthest outskirts of town. Before leaving, our neighbor *Kiliji* Hampar (mentioned above) and I went and rented a single chariot, which was supposed to carry what both of our families were taking with them. Hampar had also been given the right to accompany his family on the first stage of the deportation journey. As our caravan made its way across the bridge, a teenage boy threw himself into the lake and emerged on the other side of the waters. When he was reunited with the rest of the deportees and asked why he had jumped, he replied, laughing maniacally—"Didn't you see? A bunch of monsters were coming for us, they wanted to cut us to pieces!" and he continued cackling hysterically.

Who knew? He wasn't crazy. He was, in fact, prophesying the future.

The caravan's first stop, after leaving Sivas, was the valley at the foot of Mount Kardaghlar. There, my family was joined by my uncle Serop Apkarian's family. When the people in the caravan wanted to drink water, they were all chained together and taken to the river to satiate their thirst. However, not all of men were chained. When the people got to the river, some of these men swam across and tried to make their escape. The soldiers immediately began looking for the escapees. One of them was my uncle Serop. The family was extremely distraught, despite the fact that they all knew that his escape meant he would probably be spared death. Eventually, my maternal uncle promised the *gendarmes* who accompanied the caravan 2 *Mejids* if they found my uncle. The promise of money immediately spurred the *gendarmes* on. Within fifteen minutes, they set up a trap and recaptured my uncle, who had no choice but to rejoin the caravan. When he saw the rest of the family again, he simply said—"what was the point of trying to find me? We will be separated soon anyway . . . ."

The caravan continued its journey. After spending one night under the stars, the next morning, the policemen escorting the caravan woke everyone up and ordered them to march. Already, the summit of the nearby mountains was visible, and they represented the first stop of the caravan outside of Sivas's borders. The moment of parting had arrived, but at this point the Turks chose a few of the Armenian girls in the caravan and sent them back to the city with an escort. These women had been ordered back to the city by the son of Emir Bey, a local official, for obvious reasons. All of the girls were members of the Kondurmajian family, who lived across the street from the Aramian School.

Nearby, Hampar tearfully embraced his family, including his children, and my mother, Hunazant. It would be the last time he would see most of them.

It was now my turn. First, Shushan, who was nearby, embraced me and thanked me for defending her when the Turkish boys had attacked us many years earlier. For a moment, she and I looked into each other's eyes, and in our innocent minds, imagined all the things that may have been, had circumstances been different.

Then my mother approached me. Tears streaming down her cheeks, she kissed both of my eyes, caressed my head, and said "Good-bye, my son, take good care of yourself." I was filled with the desire to do something to whisk her away from the situation, or to go with her to protect her. But what could I do? I squeezed Nazeli's and her son Karnig's hands. And then, while I watched, the caravan scaled the Kartashlar Yokush Hill, their Golgotha, and disappeared from view. How can I ever forget that last glimpse I caught of them? After all these years, it had come to this . . . .

Hampar and I began our long, lonely walk back to town. When we crossed the bridge over the Halys River, we both went down to the banks and splashed our faces with the cold water to wash away our tears. We spent that night sleeping under the stars, because we couldn't yet reach Sivas. The next day, as soon as we got back into the city, we tried asking everyone around us if they knew the fate that had befallen the caravan. There was nothing to be done. Hampar went to the hospital to resume his duties, and I gingerly made my way to the workshop. The next few weeks were pure agony as we waited for news from our families. Eventually, we received one single letter that informed us that the caravan had reached Malatia. We never knew if the letter was genuine.

When I saw her the last time, my mother was sixty years old. My brother Hovhanness was only thirty-eight years old.

§§§

In a way, my father was the first of my family to fall victim to the brutality of the Turks, although he died after the Hamidian massacres, and not the events of 1915. During the Genocide, our family's losses included the following:

- My mother, Hunazant; my sister-in-law, Nazeli, and her son, Karnig.
- My brother, Hovhanness, his wife, Anna, and their children Souren, Murat, and Paris.
- My uncle Serop, his wife Yeghourt, and their children Teghaper, Stepan, and Bayzar. Bayzar's husband Zacharia and their three children.
- My uncle Kevork, his wife Merijan, and their two sons Vahan and Armenak.
- My uncle (on my mother's side) Nishan Apkarian (the older of my two maternal uncles), his wife Markrouhi, and their two daughters.
- My uncle (on my mother's side) Merujan Apkarian (the younger of my two maternal uncles), his wife Elbiz, and their two sons Levon and Zareh.
- My aunt (on my mother's side), Zaruk Nizamian, her husband Hampar, their son Yeremia, his wife, and their two children Vahan and Vaghenak; as well as their son Thaddeus, and his wife Rebecca. This last couple was childless.
- My aunt (on my mother's side), Noyemzar Parseghian, her husband Misak, their son Dertad, their daughter Azniv, her husband Voskan, and the latter two's daughter.
- My aunt (on my father's side) Armav Ghetertoughian and her husband, as well as their sons Asadour and Hovakim, and their two daughters.

In total, my family lost fifty-one people. Let me mention that none of these innocent victims were a member of any political party or were involved in any type of political activity. Their daily lives were spent working, taking care of their families, and doing their best to eke out an existence. Their joys were limited by their occasional family gatherings, weddings, baptisms, and other such occasions. Their only crime was being Armenian.

As for those in my family who survived—my sister, Khanoum, and my two brothers, Dikran and Kaloust, having immigrated to America before the breakout of the War, were spared. Their children, grand-children, and great-grandchildren eventually numbered more than thirty-eight. Unfortunately, the majority of them have become assim-ilated in America's great melting pot.

One of my cousins, Hagop Apkarian, having miraculously survived the deportation and massacres, ended up in Middleton, New York. His family, including children and grandchildren, numbered eighteen. Some of them, too, have lost their Armenian roots.

Another cousin of mine, Smbad Apkarian, son of Merujan, also sur-vived the Genocide somehow, and later established a home in Lebanon. He had more than a dozen children and grandchildren.

Also, an aunt on my mother's side, some relatives ended up surviving the Genocide. As if predicting the imminent disaster, a few months prior to the outbreak of the War, they had sold their homes and their properties, and alongside their children, had fled to Bulgaria, and then from there had made their way to France. The number of their children and grandchildren, some of whom eventually ended up in Marseilles, and some others who reached Chicago, passed forty.

Based on my approximate calculations, the number of survivors and their progeny from my family eventually exceeded 108. If these num-bers were to be the same for an Ottoman-Armenian population of two million, it stands to reason that there would now be more than twelve million Armenians across the world. Clearly, the Turkish government failed miserably in its plan to annihilate us.

§§§

Right around this time, the government also introduced the *Emvali Metruke* (Abandoned Properties) ordinance, under which officials were given permission to confiscate properties of Armenians who were no longer living in the city. This task was entrusted to Nuri Bey, who had once taught us Turkish at school, and to his brother Bejet *Effendi*, who had taught Turkish at the Aramian school. They were the leaders of the requisition teams that went around, cataloged the properties of Arme-nians, then supervised their transfer to the erstwhile main cathedral of Sivas, where everything was stored.

These two officials, accompanied by three or four assistants, went from home to home and from shop to shop, and made records of all the possessions that had been left behind by their denizens and owners.

Then, all of these possessions were transported to a nearby Armenian church, where they were auctioned off to the public at laughable prices. Naturally, these possessions included about ninety percent of what the local Armenians owned, which they had left behind, unable to carry it with them.

One day, I heard that it was our old neighborhood's turn to be scoured. I went there, and I witnessed Nuri Bey appear. I asked him if I could simply take a blanket from my home. "Get lost, dog!" he yelled back. He clearly knew that no Armenians would return to reclaim their property.

It was also around this time that Governor Mouammer was petitioned by some high-ranking officials, who lobbied him to allow the families of Armenians serving in the armed forces to stay. His simple reply was that what happened to the civilians was his business and his business only.

§§§

Many weeks after the deportations, one day, around noon, I ran into Yeremia Boyajian. He was a man of my age, and a former student at the Aramian School, whom I used to know. His father and my uncle Hovhanness had been in business together selling fruit, and as children, we had often played together. He looked awful, and his clothing and his shoes were in tatters. I and the other Armenian workers at the military workshop immediately surrounded him and pelted him with questions. He had been in the caravan that had left Sivas and had headed for Malatia. He told us of brutality, of murders, of rapes, of raids, and of thefts. He told us how the caravan, after reaching Malatia, hadn't even been allowed to enter the city proper but had been made to circumvent it and head for the nearby Kurdish town of Akpunak. They had spent the night there, and in the morning they had marched to Ferenjali, another small town, where they had been made to abandon their chariots and carts. They had been made to take the mountain pass, through which two men couldn't walk abreast, and eventually reached the town called Cheleb. Here, the men were separated from the group, were searched again, robbed one more time, then their arms had been bound. They had been led into a nearby valley, where they had been executed. They hadn't just been shot dead. Some had been stabbed and hacked to death with axes. I remember thinking, a man must be a monster to hack a bound man to death, a man who could offer no resistance or defense.

Apparently, in the chaos, Yeremia had been somehow able to escape and had retraced his steps to Malatia and then on to Sivas.

Then the questions really started—each man wanted to know about his family, his relatives, and his friends. I remember the scene as if it had happened yesterday—Yeremia, his back to the wall of the old Aramian school, raking his memories, trying to remember how our loved ones had died, or what state they had been in when he had last seen them.

When it was finally my turn to question him, he began without being prompted, "Last time I saw your brother Hovhanness, he was being taken away in Cheleb, alongside *Kumik* Artin. Both of them had their hands tied. I asked him where he was going, and all he said to me was—How should I know where they're taking me?"

Notes

1. From Kegh.
2. "Master" in Turkish; the word *Varbed* conveys the same meaning in Armenian.
3. From Tokat.

5

Life in the Army

By July 1915, the only Armenians left in Sivas were those who were soldiers, apostates, and who knew crafts that were valuable to the Ottoman government. There was usually only one Armenian survivor from each profession. Among these was Merujan Odabashian, the owner of the city's *Bon Marche* market. He was a personal friend of Governor Mouammer's. Other such Armenians included the governor's personal barber; The Enkabadian brothers, who were official government photographers; and Kapikian Hajji, the painter. His brother was deported, and thanks to his survival, we know much about what happened to the Armenians who left Sivas. On the other hand, other prominent Armenians who should have been saved by their statures, but who were deported, included the tailors Hagop and Rodeos, *Sobanji* Bedik, Vahan Jenlian, and the cloth merchant Lertoghian, as well as the brothers Rodeos and Yervant.

§§§

Months passed, and those Armenians who were serving the army kept waiting for news from the caravan. We only received occasional missives, written in Turkish, asking about the men's health and also asking for money. Since I knew how to read and write Turkish, I was able to read and respond to all of my fellow soldiers' letters, quickly ingratiating myself with all of them. I often also read letters, ostensibly, by Armenians who had been deported, to their relatives who served at the workshop. The letters seemed fake and always asked for money to be sent. I was always able to take advantage of my talents to survive, and by this point, I was fluent in Armenian, Turkish, and French, to which I would later add English, when I moved to the United States. But for now, my knowledge of languages allowed me to make myself essential within my own division. I didn't provide this service just to the Armenian soldiers, either. Many of the Turkish troops were illiterate and asked me to help them read or write letters. Often, when writing for Armenian soldiers, despite the fact that

Alexanian with the bugle that saved his life.

I never expected my colleagues' families to respond to their letters, I would slip in a line asking about my own family, hoping against hope that these people would answer and would provide me information regarding what had happened to them. Unfortunately, I never heard anything about them.

The men I served with were simple creatures. One of them, a small portly man, once asked me not only to read him a letter but also to block my ears so I wouldn't hear what I was reading.

Unfortunately, I was not a particularly skilled tailor, especially when working with antiquated, second-hand machines. I often had trouble meeting my daily production quota. Thankfully, my compatriots serving with me were always willing to lend me a hand and work extra hours to help me.

One day, the workshop was visited by the commander of the twenty-seventh Division, Commander Adni. He mentioned the fact that the workshop had no bugler. He was told by Commander Cherkez Isak Bey, who was in charge of 1,000 soldiers and was Commander Ethim's replacement, that the higher echelon had never made an issue out of the absence of a bugler, but Commander Adni was not satisfied with the excuse. As soon as he left, Commander Isak Bey turned to Lieutenant Hamdi Chavoush and ordered him to find a bugler. The latter tried to find someone who could fill the position, and I eventually built up the courage to nominate myself.

"You Armenians!" he murmured, "you stick your noses in everything! But . . . You can give it a try, if you want . . ."

On the designated day, eight to ten Turkish troops were present and were asked to show what they could do, and none of them had the faintest idea how to play the bugle. Most of them simply turned red blowing as hard as they could.

"Damn!" called out an officer from nearby, "it'll take us months to teach these dolts how to play a simple note! What are we going to tell the commander when he comes to visit next time?"

At that point, the lieutenant whispered something into his orderly's ear, who fetched me. Embarrassed by all the eyes that were trained on me, I immediately picked up the bugle and played a tune. The officer came down to me, and slapping my shoulder said, "Good job, my son!" then, turning back to the other officers, added—"From now on, this boy will not have to do anything other than blow the bugle!" He even told them that I was allowed to leave the workshop and the barracks during my free time.

It took me only a few days to learn the calls on an old bugle, and I was appointed as the official bugler of my Division. Most of all, I was happy that I would no longer have to meet the impossible quotas that were imposed on the tailors of the workshop. Also, now that I had a lot of free time, I started helping my fellow soldiers by running errands for them in town.

§§§

One day—and I say one day because at the time, we lived like slaves waiting for our death sentence, and we simply had given up keeping track of the days—we were told that on the occasion of a Bayram, we would have the day off from work. I'm not sure if it was the Muslim New Year or the birthday of the sultan, but either way, we were told we would not have to work on that day. We were sitting around the *gharavana*, which was a kind of large bowl that they served food to soldiers in, and we were lapping up the meat and potatoes that the *gharavana* contained. There were eight of us, and our officer, all eating out of the same bowl. It was a hot day in 1916, halfway through the war. We had just finished our meal when the commanding officer of the workshop, Lieutenant Ethem *Effendi*, walked by and entered his quarters, the erstwhile kindergarten building of the defunct Armenian school.

At the time, there were Armenian soldiers who were choosing to commit suicide, like Massis Odabashian, unable to make peace with the new world in which they found themselves. Others had lost their minds as they struggled to find their identities. The majority, confused by the torrent of orders and edicts that were issued on an almost daily basis, bade their time and tried to survive. At the same time, these men never shirked their duties as soldiers of the Ottoman Army. This was the general situation of almost all Armenians serving at the Sivas workshop. Sure, we had been spared the deportations, but death hung like a Damoclean Sword over us every minute of our lives.

Then, suddenly, a miracle! It was as if it was message from the Gods. The earth shook, and we all fell from our seats. It was an earthquake! The Lieutenant, white as a ghost, ran out of his room in a panic, slipped, and falling hard onto his face, swallowed a mouthful of dirt! I'm sure he never forgot the fact that he was so severely humiliated before a bunch of *geyavours*.

§§§

Another few months passed, and one night, news that the Russians had taken Erzincan reached Sivas, and spread with the speed of a wildfire. All Army divisions were asked to hand over a list of "suspicious" Armenians in the ranks of the soldiers to higher authorities. These Armenian soldiers were seen as potential fifth column and now had to be dealt with. In fact, right after the fall of Erzincan, I overheard two Turkish soldiers talking. One of them, answering a question from his colleague as to what would now happen to the Armenians, replied "Well, I assume we're now going to have to kill them all so they won't take revenge on us."

One day, during our lunch break on a bright spring day in 1916, Hamdi Chavoush came to our mess hall, and announced that after the meal, twenty of the Armenian troops were to line up against the building that had once served as a kindergarten to the Aramian School. He said it was the commander's order. He read the names out, and mine was one of them. There we all lined up, in two rows. One row comprised the educated Armenian soldiers, including myself, and the other comprised the uneducated ones. Regardless, these were all the best craftsmen of the city, ranging from seventeen to seventy years of age. They had all been working nonstop since the outbreak of hostilities to produce the boots and uniforms that Turkish troops wore on the front, without receiving any payment for their toils. Among those who had lined up were *Ousda* Ohan, *Ekkarents* Nazar, Melkon Chadijian, Yeghik Penikian, Sarkis Ohnikian, Sarkis Basmajian and his brother, Master Yervant *Khavertsents*, Antranik Alexanian, Hagop Chatijian (who was a master machinist at the Singer company's headquarters in the city), Armenak Dumanian (the head of the Armenian *Bartevagoump* scouting troupe and who had been working as an accountant in the workshop's offices), and Armenak Aslanian, who had the same job and was the son of Voskan Aslanian, a former government functionary. Others who were there included Kerop from Tokat, Daniel, Dertad, Yervant Katsakhian, and others from outside Sivas, including from Marzevan. As I have already said, these men had been working without pay for the Ottoman Army for more than two years, having been separated forever from their families by their own

Another Armenian who served in the Ottoman Army warehouse in Sivas, Jirair Ferhatian, who had been a pharmacist before the war.

63

employers. They had kept their heads down, not even knowing where their wives and children had been buried, and now they had no idea what awaited them.

Ethem *Effendi* came outside inspected the twenty Armenians who had lined up, then, calling over his adjutant, told him to take me and Armenak Aslanian out of the group. I believe the only reason I was singled out and saved was because I knew how to play the bugle, and had they killed me, the workshop would have been left without a bugler. The remaining eighteen men were taken away, including one of my friends, a man called Hoomo. Three days later, when I went out into the city, I saw their blood-soaked clothes being sold in the market.

When I look back on the years I spent at the workshop, I remember Hoomo, one of those who died that day, with particular fondness. His full name was Hoomayak Odabashian, and he was a big, husky, and tall young man. The boys called him Hoomo for short. He had all the looks of a wrestler, arms and hands like a tiger's, yet a heart so gentle, so mellow that he would not dare hurt even a fly. Hoomo was a model soldier, a good worker, and liked by all because he had respect for everybody, young and old. He was admitted at the military workshop by the usual application, which was somehow lost in the records, and therefore he was deprived of every day's meal until the application was found and officially admitted.

Meal or no meal, Hoomo would not dare open his mouth fearing that he would be taken out to be deported and massacred like the rest of the Armenians forced to leave home. The spring of 1915 brought us together, working in the same tailoring department where we used to produce uniforms using the Singer sewing machines the government confiscated from a local company's warehouse. These machines needed plenty of oil and quite strong legs to operate. After supper, we used to sit under a tree in the courtyard of the workshop and chat.

Hoomo had actually been a pupil in the Aramian School from childhood up and had been only one year away from graduation when the war had broken out. The two of us would sit in the courtyard, and he would talk about his school days, while I would talk about mine. Also, he knew all about the Armenian songs and hymns, which gave me a great deal of pleasure to learn. We would end our meetings by beginning to sing *Kna Boulboul mer Ashkharen*,[1] but then in a moment or two, we would stop, unable to finish the song. Tears would roll down our cheeks, and we would retire to our cots.

Two days after his execution with the other men, as I was out shopping, I saw with my own eyes, Hoomo's clothes offered for sale stained with his young, innocent blood, the purest blood I have known. That was the reward the Turks could offer to those innocent Armenians who served the country for over two years without any pay, except one pound of bread and a handful of bulgur every twenty-four hours.

This coincided with another terrible event—3,000–4,000 young Armenian men, who had been forced to work in road construction, were executed near the city. Basically, the Ottoman government was finally executing its plan of annihilation.

§§§

The following Friday was a holiday, and the Turkish troops had been given leave to visit their homes. Only the Armenian soldiers remained in the workshop, eating together in the courtyard. The lieutenant asked to see me and ordered me to summon all the Armenian troops to his quarters after the meal. When we were all gathered, the lieutenant announced that an order had come from the top, saying that no Armenians were allowed to serve in the Ottoman army henceforth.

He proceeded to explain that the only chance we Armenian troops had of survival lay in our conversion to Islam. After a few minutes of thinking, as we demurred, he added: "We have received an order saying no more Armenians will be allowed to stay within our ranks. There's only one way for you all to survive—you've got to become Muslims and accept the prophet into your hearts. There is no other way. You have twenty-four hours to respond. You have to choose between life and death. You must swallow this camel and become apostates, or you will no longer be of this world. That's all. If you refuse to convert, you'd better pray that the enemy never steps foot in this land, because if they do, it'll be over your dead bodies. You have twenty-four hours."

We were dismissed and went back to our cots. I don't think any of us got any sleep. We spent the night praying and seeking guidance from God. Even some of our Turkish colleagues had tears in their eyes—after all, for them, too, the idea of becoming apostates was reprehensible. By the next morning, we had decided—unable to resist the threats of the lieutenant, all but seven of the Armenians soldiers had decided to convert to Islam. Only I and six others stood firm and refused.

Sometime later, the remaining four of us who had refused conversion, including myself, were asked to see the lieutenant again. Without mincing his words, he addressed me, as he considered me to be the most articulate of the troops there, and asked me why we had decided to remain Christian. He wondered why healthy, young men would sign their own death sentences and refuse a conversion that would save their lives.

"No," I replied, "after seeing my mother, brother, sister-in-law, and my whole family die, and after serving in the same army that killed them, is death what I deserve? If the Sultan, in clear conscience, can kill this many faithful soldiers, then let that weigh on his soul. I've been ready to die since the day I lost my family."

I turned to my comrades, and added—"You should be of my mentality!" None protested.

The lieutenant was taken aback.

"Get out of my sight!" was his only response.

All of us left, refusing to convert. I knew, as I left the room, that if the Russians ever made it to Sivas, we would all be summarily executed. As if to reinforce this message, just around this time, about 200 Armenian soldiers, many of them from Marzevan, were brought through the barracks. They were ordered to line up against the wall of what had once been the kindergarten building of the Aramian School, after which they were led out to their execution.

§§§

By this point, being the only bugler at the workshop, my schedule was very light—I was woken up by the guards at 6:00 a.m., and I blew the bugle summoning everyone to work at 6:30 a.m. I also had to signal the beginning and end of the lunch breaks. I had some idle time between the morning and the noon, which I spent running errands for the commander and older soldiers. I would go buy *shish kebobs*, lamb's heads, cheese, and yogurt. These were delicacies for them, since they neither had the time nor were allowed to leave the workshop. They had to spend their entire days producing clothing and shoes for the Turkish soldiers.

One day, an officer asked me to buy yogurt. As I was strolling in the *maydan*, which was a large square where local farmers sold their produce and products, I spotted an elderly Turkish peasant sitting on the ground. There was only a single Armenian farmer in the square that day, as all the Armenian villages of the area had already been emptied,

The Main Square (maydan) of Sivas.

their livestock confiscated, their men killed on the spot, and women and children uprooted and sent into the deserts of Syria to die. The Turkish villager had some eggs, butter, cheese, and only one container of yogurt—in a copper pot. I asked him how much he wanted for the yogurt, and he asked for a fair price but I was thinking of how to carry the yogurt, as I had no container, no bottle, and nothing to pour the yogurt into. I told the old farmer that I wished to buy the yogurt, but I had no way to carry it. He looked up and said, "Just pay me, and I will trust that you will return the pot. May the men who caused so much misfortune to your people go blind."

Here was a Turkish man trusting me with a pot that was worth at least six times the price of its contents. I hurried to the workshop. I carried it to the barracks, had the yogurt dumped into a bag, and hurried back to return the copper pot. This time the farmer was in tears. He looked up and said, "Son, didn't I tell you you would return it?"

This event immediately reminded me of something else I had witnessed some years prior, in Sivas. There was a young Turk there, named *Kel* Gobi. They had nicknamed him *Kel*, because in his young age, through some sickness, he had lost his hair, in other words he was bald. This young Turk was the curse of the city. A loafer, he made a living by swindling, especially the farmers. Nothing could stop him. The prison was almost his permanent home.

One day he spotted a Turkish farmer discussing the price of some fresh butter filled in a wooden container. *Kel* Gobi butted in, and he said to the farmer that he also wanted to bid on the butter. On the farmer's refusal to sell it to him, as he knew him well by reputation, he grabbed the container filled with butter, and said to the farmer, "How come you want to sell your butter to an Armenian, an infidel, and not to a Muslim?" He commanded the farmer to stay where he was as he would return the empty container.

Sure enough, he returned with the empty container and asked the farmer to follow him. They went to a nearby store to weigh the wooden container. The poor farmer was waiting and asking for his money for the butter. In response, *Kel* Gobi turned to the farmer and said "*Eshek*[2] Kurd, what money do you want from me? I took the butter, and now I'm giving you the container, which is worth six pounds. You owe me the difference." The poor farmer picked up his container crying. "Didn't I tell you I didn't want to sell you anything?" he asked. Here was a Turkish man who would rather do business with Armenians rather than Turks, because he trusted Armenians more.

§§§

Once I became the army workshop's bugler, and had time to kill, I began running errands for the other men serving with me, both Armenians and Turks. After all, I had much more free time than they did, and many of them had helped me meet my production quotas. Also, on Fridays, the Muslim day of rest, we were allowed to leave the barracks. An officer would gather all the troops who wanted to leave the workshop and would lead them out. It was forbidden for the soldiers to drink alcohol or to consort with women. The soldiers would be arranged in square formation, lined up in fours, and would advance through the streets chanting martial songs. Pedestrians always saluted us when they saw us passing. One day, as I crossed a street at a trot, my bugle tucked under my arm, and as I was passing a group of people on the side of the road, I suddenly did a double take. My attention was focused on that group—three or four Turkish women, their faces covered by silk veils, were walking with another woman, a bit shorter than the rest, and whose face was half-uncovered. For some reason, I had a suspicion that the shorter woman was Armenian. Just at that moment, the girl's eyes fell on me, and she stumbled to the ground, her eyes still fixed on me. As she lost her balance and fell, I rushed to her aid. As soon as I helped her up and had seen her up close, I exclaimed "Shushan!" but immediately recovered my wits, turned back, and returned to the barracks, where I was almost late to blow the postmeal bugle. Right afterward, I slipped out of the barracks again, and running down the road, I found the group of Turkish women, but then did not know what to do. They were all in a house, and I could see Shushan through the crack of the door, which had been left ajar. Shushan, seeing me, whispered, "Yervant, help me!"

"Be brave, Shushan, don't be afraid!" I whispered back.

From the inside, the women summoned Shushan, who shut the door and disappeared inside. I loitered about, my thoughts in turmoil, hoping to see Shushan's face one more time, but to no avail. I thought of somehow slipping her a note, but what if the note fell into the wrong hands? I returned to the barracks, my head hanging low, not seeing a solution to this new problem I was faced with. Regardless of how I did it, I considered it my responsibility to rescue Shushan out of the clutches of her Turkish masters, being well aware of how the Turks used young Armenian girls. That evening, when most of the other troops were spending their only leisure time in songs, dances, and revelry, I stayed in a corner, lost in my thoughts. The others, sensing my dejection, couldn't help but tease, "What are you so sad about? You scared of something?" asked one.

"How would you feel if like us, you had lost your own children to the deportations, huh?" asked another.

"Hmm . . . He's just scared for his life. You should've just become an apostate if you are so afraid . . . Maybe that would have saved you . . . But too late now . . . ."

"Leave me alone, please . . . ." I implored, and jumping to my feet, left the barracks.

The next day, a new edict was issued, announcing that henceforth, Armenian troops could only leave the barracks on Fridays, and then only with special permission. And so, I was forced to endure almost an entire week in the barracks with the other soldiers, waiting impatiently for Friday. Finally the day came, and having received permission, I ran out of the gate. I immediately headed for the house in which I had seen Shushan, but when I arrived, I found the house abandoned and empty. I inquired with some of the neighbors, who all told me they thought the residents of the house had left for Istanbul only two days earlier. In despair, I found myself wandering about the market area, where I soon noticed one of my old teachers from school, who had also been serving in the army, selling books and stationery.

"What is all this, Mr. Harutyun?" I asked, "Are you selling all your books and writing implements?"

"What can I do?" he answered, "there's a new edict that Armenian soldiers who are still here must soon go to Istanbul, where they have to receive more training and be sent to the front. Why don't you try to go to Istanbul, too, and enroll in the academy? You know it's a lot safer there . . . ."

"No, I'd rather stay here . . . ."

"Why? Are you crazy? What for? You have an opportunity now to leave this God-forsaken place. There is life out there."

"Brother," I responded, "life holds no value to me now."

"Enough! We have no time for that rubbish. Yervant, listen to me, become a Turk, then sign up to be sent to Istanbul. Within a week, you will be sent to the capital."

The repeated hearing of "Istanbul" shook me up. I suddenly realized that going to Istanbul may actually offer me the opportunity to find Shushan. The next day, I went into the government offices and officially became an apostate. The process of conversion was very simple—and all I had to do was sign a paper, attesting that I was now a Muslim.

"Good, my son," said the officer who performed the conversion, smiling, "your new name will be Zia, since you finally saw the light. You will be much freer now, much happier. And you already know how to read and write Turkish."

Within a few days, I was given the permission to go to Istanbul. My commander was a bit upset—after all, he was losing his only bugler. Unfortunately, we couldn't go straight to the capital. First, we were sent to a military training camp in the northern part of Sivas, called Kazak Yagh. The training camp had once been a hospital, but it had recently been converted. It had been built by Armenian workers, who had been murdered since. This was still in June 1916. We stayed there for a month, for training, until July 1916.

Eventually, I left with three others—Sarkis Ansourian, his brother Hrant, who eventually went to Yerevan, and Mihran Baliozian. These were three Armenian officers who were being sent to Istanbul with me. We made our way over the Cherji Keres Mountain. We spent the time talking to each other and occasionally to other travelers. One of them, the caravan guide, showed us the mouth of a deep cavern, where he said many Armenians had been dumped and eventually killed. The cavern had then been sealed with a large boulder and some dirt. The travelers, mortified, looked on it in horror. The caravan driver asked why everyone was so upset, after all, they were just Armenians . . . . He told the story with a perverted sort of pride and relish.

My companions had to restrain me from jumping on the man . . . . I could not control myself and wanted to attack him . . . . That well may have been my own mother's resting place . . .

Eventually we arrived in Erekli, where I boarded a train for the first time in my life. The train took us to a station past Ismid. From there, we made our way to the military academy that was our destination. The academy was called the *Pera Harbie*,[3] located in the Pera District[4] of Istanbul, very close to Taksim Square. When we reached Istanbul, we were all held up, including myself, and we had to be inoculated before we entered the capital. While I was coming out of the shower, in the long line of people, near the gate, I was spotted by a tall Turk with a long beard. I heard him holler, "Hey! There is a *geyavour* in this line!"

He started to follow me, and I ran fast, very fast, and hid behind a big machine that was disinfecting our clothing. I dressed very quickly, and walked out toward the train waiting to take me to Haydar Pasha. I could see that tall Turk still looking for me as the train pulled out of the station.

At the academy, we soon took our entrance examinations alongside many of the sons of rich Turks and high-ranking government officials. Seven Armenians were in my class, along with Kamil Pasha Zade Mujafar Effendi, who was purportedly Enver's brother-in-law. Also, two of my teachers from the Jesuit school, Khachadour Fenerjian and Harutyun Zaratzian, had graduated from this academy. We passed our examinations, and on that same exact day were given new uniforms and weapons, and our training began. I was eventually to be trained in the use of artillery and machine guns and was to be sent to the Dardanelles, where a division had been wiped out by the allies. I soon received my rank as a second lieutenant at the institute. Before being sent to the Dardanelles, I was stationed in Melemon near Smyrna, where I was responsible for the officers' mess and for procurements, including supplies and uniforms. I once served dinner to a famous Armenian high-ranking officer named Levon Ajemian, who was a doctor. I would later find out that he would become the father of the noted pianist Maro Ajemian and her sister, the violinist Anahid Ajemian.

Afterward, I was sent to the Dardanelles for six months. From there, I was sent to a training camp called Karshu Yaka to be trained in shooting a machine gun before being sent to the front lines. The training was supposed to last six months. Thankfully, the Armistice was declared in November 1918, and I was spared from being sent into combat.

Notes

1. "Be gone from our world, nightingale."
2. An insult roughly equivalent to "you idiot" (literally "jackass").
3. "Harbie" means "of war."
4. The Pera District is now called Beyoğlu.

6

Istanbul

My first task, after arriving in Istanbul, was to ascertain where Shushan lived. Eventually, I found her—she lived in a three-story home on the corner of a street, at the very top of a hill. One day, I was loitering outside of the house, trying to build up the courage to walk up to the door and knock. Suddenly, I turned around and saw a girl approaching the house with a stick across her shoulders and a bag at each end of the stick. The girl was Shushan, but I could not afford to reveal to the locals that I was trying to rescue her. Instead, I nonchalantly walked alongside her, with Shushan awed and amazed at this turn of events. As we walked, we had the opportunity to speak, and she told me of how she had been taken into the house where she lived, and the son of the owners of that house, sometime before, had attempted to force himself on her. She was very reluctant to elaborate, afraid that I would get angry and act out on my anger. I then gave her the address of a relative in town, as well as every single dime I had in my pocket, telling her to run away to that address, and that she would be safe there.

A strange thing happened at that moment—she looked at me with grateful eyes and asked if I loved her. At the time, I was so flushed that I told her we'd have plenty of time to talk of such things later, and I let her question hang in the air.

But I didn't notice the two *gendarmes* at the end of the street, who were watching my every move. They walked up to me now, and stopping me, asked for my name, the name of my commanding officer, and where I was stationed. I showed them my papers, which allowed me to leave my barracks on that day, at which point one of the *gendarmes* remarked that in another five minutes the leave order would expire and that I would be in contravention of military regulations. Freeing myself from their grasp with some difficulty, I sprinted toward the ferry that would take me back to the other side of the city, where the barracks were.

As I got to the ferry, the whistle sounded, and the ferry's ramp began rising. I had to take a running start and jump into the ferry, in

Yervant Alexanian graduating from the military academy with the rank of second lieutenant, with his bugle hanging from the wall nearby.

the process colliding with an officer already onboard. I had to stand at attention, salute, and offer profuse apologies.

The following Friday, while most of the troops were engaged in cleaning their weapons, an officer once again asked if any of the troops wanted to leave the base. However, I was told that I could not leave. The *gendarmes* had informed the officer of my meeting with the "girl on the street," and I was now being punished for it. I protested that the

Ottoman Army Officers training men in the use of machine guns at the military training camp of Karshu Yaka (Senekerimian Brigade pictured).

girl wasn't just a stranger, but someone I had known in my hometown. The other soldiers chuckled when they heard this statement, and the officer stated that because I had dared use that defense, I would not be allowed to leave the base for a whole month.

§§§

During my service in the army, I encountered Enver Pasha,[1] the Minister of War, a total of three times. I met him first when he went through Sivas on his way to the Russian Front. I was working at Hajinlian's store at the time, and I saw him walk right down the road. While at the front, he was wounded. He was carried away to safety from the battlefield by an Armenian lieutenant named Hovannes Aginian. As a reward, this man's entire family was deported and perished. The second time I saw Enver was at the military workshop in Sivas, on an inspection tour, after which the erstwhile Erzincan sewing unit was transferred to Sivas, as Erzincan was already in Russian hands. This also meant that command of the workshop was passed from Ethem *Effendi*, who was only in charge of 100 men, to Cherkez Isak Bey, who had 1,000 men under him. He was surrounded by high-ranking officers and accompanied by the Governor of Sivas. I met Enver for the third time in Melemon near Smyrna where I was in charge of the officers' mess. This time he came in the company of Liman von Sanders[2] and other renowned officers. They were there to inspect the sixty-first Division, which was assigned to replace another army division at the Dardanelles after the latter had been torn to pieces in combat. I was told that they would have a meal with our division, and at the time, I was responsible for the officers' mess. Oh, how I was anxious to serve them a good meal . . . . Perhaps their last one . . . . When I realized I would come into close contact with their food, I thought of poisoning the meal, and I almost put that plan into motion, but I had to remind myself that if I had

A photograph of Armenian officers in Istanbul who served in Alexanian's division. Standing from left to right: Haig Ermabeyikian (Turkish name Fauk); Toros Boodakian (Turkish name Vehmi). Seated from left to right: Sumpat Avazanian (Turkish name Selim); Levon Boodakian (Turkish name Lutfi).

assassinated Enver Pasha, I would not have been the only one paying the price for the act. Every remaining Armenian soldier in the division would probably be put to the sword. I even spoke of my plans to some of my compatriots who were there. They all recommended that I forget all about it, since many still thought there was a chance they would be reunited with their loved ones. Eventually, Enver and his consort took their meal alone, in their special train car in which they had traveled. It only had a locomotive pulling one wagon. Later, as he was leaving, I served *tan*[3] to him. After looking at the drink in my hands for a while, he took the glass, and asked –

"Oh, are we to drink *tan*?"

"It's just a farmer's treat . . . ." I replied, perhaps attempting a subtle insult. He and his retinue did not stay for lunch and soon disappeared.

The graduation ceremony of 12th class of the Pera Harbie in Istanbul, from which Alexanian also graduated.

Not too long after this event, I was sent to the Dardanelles, to Çanakkale, and my squad was meant to replace others that had been torn apart during the combat there. My commander was the German Colonel Goumero, who worked with his assistant, Goumo.

§§§

After graduating as a second lieutenant from the military academy, I was stationed in Melemon, near Smyrna. There, I witnessed more pogroms and massacres of Armenians, in full view of Western troops. I saw with my own eyes Armenians jump into the sea and swim toward the Allied battleships stationed offshore, which represented Christian nations, thinking the ships would save them. Unfortunately, this could not be further from the truth. In fact, many of the battleships turned on their hot-water hoses to keep these poor souls away, causing them to drown. Only a Japanese battleship was willing to throw down the rope ladder and rescue Armenians.

After Smyrna, I spent some time in the Dardanelles. I was there for six months, during which I received my commission as a full lieutenant, but the official papers were never signed. I was then transferred back to a training camp in Istanbul called Karshu Yaka for six months of training in machine gunnery. However, thankfully, before completing my training, news spread that the Armistice was declared. From the roof of our barracks, I and many other soldiers watched the allied battleships enter

Souvenir de Smyrne   Vue générale du Port avec le Mont Pagus

Smyrna, where Alexanian was stationed after receiving supplementary training in Istanbul.

The Ansourian Brothers, who attended Pera Harbie with Alexanian. Sarkis, whose Turkish name was Zeki, is seated and Hrant, whose Turkish name was Nouri, is standing.

the Sea of Marmara. This signaled the end of the war. I later saw the allies landing on the beaches and the British soldiers marching through the streets of Istanbul, led by a pole bearer holding aloft a British flag.

I served with quite a few Armenians in the military academy, which was by no means attended by Turks alone. The Ansoorian brothers were two of these Armenians. They had also converted, and their names had been Turkified. They, and many of the other Armenians I served with, greatly helped me ensure the years I spent serving in the Ottoman Army.

Picture of Karshu Yaka training camp—Alexanian is in light-colored uniform seated behind the machine gun on the right.

Gradually, the Ottoman troops were demobilized. As soon as a letter came for me, announcing that I would be demobilized, I went downstairs to the office and demanded my discharge papers. I was honorably discharged into the reserves on December 20, 1918. I had served a total of three and a half years in the Ottoman Army, but still, I was in the reserves, which meant that I could be called back up to the army if another war were to start. As soon as I received the discharge papers, I wasted no time changing my name back to its original Armenian, just as my Armenian colleagues all did, and of course, I recanted my conversion. I spent that night at the home of a cousin. At this time, I was still trying to figure out how to proceed. I considered traveling to Adana and getting a job as a police officer, since I had military training. I wrote to my old schoolmaster, Pere de Lavernette, who was in Adana at the time, and I told him of my plans. He discouraged me from traveling to Adana, saying that there were no jobs to be had there, and life was difficult. It was great hearing from him again, and he expressed his joy at the knowledge of my still being alive, as well as his sadness for the deaths of many of the students and teachers of my old school. Eventually, I decided to stay in Istanbul. I found myself penniless, and I was unemployed for about six months. Thankfully, Dikran Biledjian found me a job as a bookkeeper, with an Armenian tobacconist named Misak Missirian.

Notes

1. Ismail Enver Pasha (1881–1922) was a leader of the Young Turk Revolution, and later served as the Minister of War of the Ottoman Empire during World War I. He is often considered to be one of the architects of the Armenian Genocide.
2. *Generalleutnant* Otto Liman von Sanders was a German military commander who served under the flag of the Ottoman Empire during World War I.
3. Or "dough," a yogurt-based beverage popular in the Near East.

7

America

Early one morning, while I was engaged in closing the account of the previous day at work, I unexpectedly received a letter from my brother Kaloust, who lived in the United States. One can imagine how happy I was. I tore the envelope open with tears in my eyes. In the letter, my brother expressed his joy that I had escaped the deportations, told me that he would help me with any financial issues I had, and asked about my health. Soon, I also received another letter, this time from my sister in the United States, which contained a check for $20. I was overjoyed. I kissed the letters and began pacing up and down the store, my coworkers congratulating me heartily. Two months later, I received another letter from my brother, containing another check for $20 and also informing me that he was making arrangements for me to immigrate to the United States. My brother wanted me to travel right away and also hoped I could find him a bride from the old country, as he wanted to remarry, since

The Souirah, which took Alexanian and Keushkerian from Istanbul to Marseilles.

his wife Nazeli and son Karnig had been killed during the Genocide. Although I had been separated from my brother for eight years, I did my best to ask around, gather some information regarding potential wives, and sent this information to him. I even visited several orphanages to find young Armenian girls, but Kaloust would not approve any of them. I also sent pictures, as well as my observations regarding each of their personalities. During this time, by coincidence, I met an impoverished local woman, who, alongside her daughter, barely eked out a living washing whites for the city's public hospital. When I mentioned that my brother was looking for a bride, the poor woman, having heard of the wealth of America, and hoping to provide her daughter with a better life, suggested her as a candidate. I was not sure, since the girl was barely eighteen years old and my brother was much older, but the woman replied to this objection by saying that she, too, had married an older man at the same age and that older men are more likely to appreciate a good woman. I agreed to send a picture of this girl to my brother too, and less than a month later, the latter sent me $500 for the two of us to travel to America. Her name was Marie Keushkerian.

A photograph taken in Marseilles, showing Marie Keushkerian and her betrothed Kaloust.

Passports were ordered, preparations were made, and the farewells were said. Our first ship, the Souirah, left Istanbul at 3:00 p.m. on October 27, 1920.

The first few days of the trip proceeded smoothly, and I did my best to see to the needs of the girl who was my charge. Four days into the journey, the ship sailed by Italy, and those on board could see the glittering lights of the shore. It was one of those magical nights, when the countless stars twinkled in the heavens and were reflected on Earth by the millions of lights of the city. After dinner, most of the passengers, accompanied by their husbands, wives, or lovers, were on the bridge, admiring the scenery. I and the girl, too, were huddled in a corner, telling each other our stories and consoling each other with plans for the future. We had both lived through terrible tribulations back home. On the fifth day of the journey, the seas were rougher, and I was soon seasick and was restricted to my cabin. Not wanting to bother Marie with thoughts of me, and not wanting her to feel obligated to nurse me, I made my way, despite being half-conscious, to the kitchens where I ate what I could. However, Marie noticed that I was sick and nursed me back to health, afraid she would have to continue the journey alone. Then, a few days later, huge swells rocked the ship, which soon became filled with water. I, despairingly, told her, after making sure she was provided with a floating vest, to pass on my greetings to my brother and the others, thinking I would not make it, since they would probably only have time to rescue women and children. Her response was that she refused to leave without me and that she preferred drowning at sea to going to America by herself. Thankfully, around dawn, the storm subsided, and around that noon, the ship made its entry into the port of Marseille. We arrived in Marseilles on November 2, 1920. The two of us stayed at a hotel in the city, called the Hotel Prince, waiting for our next ship.

One night, the two of us went to a nearby cafe, where we sat talking.

"Do you think life will be good in America? Do you think I will have a happy marriage?" Marie asked.

"I don't see why you wouldn't," I replied.

"But how can you be so sure? After all, I'm going into an arranged marriage. I don't know your brother, except for what you have told me. I have no idea what kind of a person he is. And, don't forget, there's a big difference in age . . . ."

"It is up to you whether you go through with this marriage or not. I, too, don't have much faith in these arranged marriages. You will make up your mind once you arrive."

"No . . . But I can't do it that quickly. I can't just wed as soon as I get there. If only I knew what kind of a person he is . . . If you tell me he's like you, you'll set my mind at ease . . . ."

"Well, I'm his younger brother, and the young always learn from the old, right?"

"That's how it used to be, but times have changed now . . . ."

"It's late tonight . . . ." I said as a clock began chiming somewhere. "Tomorrow we'll have all day to discuss this . . . ."

§§§

Our plan was to leave Marseille as soon as possible. But we were stuck in the city for a whole month. Finally, we were able to reserve our cabins on the SS Zeeland, which belonged to the American Red Star Line, and left from Cherbourg. The ship left on December 3, 1920.

On December 13, 1920, at 10:00 a.m. the ship docked in New York Harbor. We had to spend the first night on the ship itself, and the next morning, without any trouble, we were able to clear customs and were released from Ellis Island. However, right as we got our passports stamped, the customs officer asked us if we were a couple. I responded by explaining that Marie would soon become the wife of my brother. The officer then unceremoniously informed us that if she was traveling to become a bride in the United States, she had to wed within two weeks of her arrival in order not to be considered an illegal alien.

Naturally, we had quite a bit of difficulty orienting ourselves, this being our first time in New York City. We would have had even more difficulty, had we not come across an Armenian man, whom we met by accident, and who was a tour guide. He made sure we took the right train, and we soon arrived at 159 East 27th Street, where my brother had his hotel and restaurant.

There were warm scenes of reunion, and soon night began to fall, at which point we got ready to go upstairs, but then my sister Khanoum arrived from Bridgeport, Connecticut. We talked long into that night

Anvers. — S/S « ZEELAND » de la Red Star Line.

The SS Zeeland, which took Alexanian to the United States.

around the dinner table. There was so much to discuss. We spoke of what had happened to our family, how I had escaped death, my experiences in the Army, and what had happened to Sivas in the time my brother had been away from it.

§§§

Marie was nervous when we arrived at my brother's house. That first night, she excused herself from the table before dinner was over and went upstairs to the room that had been given to her. Noticing her absence, I followed her upstairs, and I saw her sitting on the bed, in a disconsolate state. She was staring at a framed picture in the room showing Kaloust and his deceased wife and son. I asked her what was wrong, and she explained to me that she was now reluctant to marry Kaloust—he had, after all, a family already. I could do nothing but console her and told her that she still had two weeks to make up her mind and that she should do whatever she felt was right.

Yervant Alexanian at the age of 25, when he first came to the United States.

Unfortunately, Marie had no other choice. She couldn't even fathom making the trip back to Istanbul, alone on a ship. She decided to go ahead with the wedding. Two days later, she and Kaloust were married at the New York City Hall. Aside from the justice of peace and the two of them, only three people were present to witness their union—myself, my sister Khanoum, and an Armenian priest.

Afterward, I stayed with Kaloust for a while, until I was able to find a job and get back on my feet. Only a few years later, in 1924, at the age of 36, Kaloust died in Bridgeport, Connecticut, leaving behind his widow, Marie, and their son Nishan.

Afterword

Yervant Alexanian, after all of his trials and tribulations, established himself in the United States and began prospering. In 1920, when he first landed in the New World, he intended to become a French teacher at the high school or college level, but, not having the luxury of time, since his siblings who had immigrated to the United States before him needed his financial help, instead ended up getting a job at the B. Altman Department Store as a tailor. Meanwhile, he endeavored to perfect his English, receiving a graduation diploma from P.S. 55 in the Bronx on October 13, 1932, making English the fourth language that he was fluent in, after Armenian, Turkish, and French. Yervant received his certificate of American citizenship on August 15, 1929.

Later in life, between 1924 and the mid-1930s, Yervant had already found some success. He owned two dry cleaning and tailor shops in Bronx and one in Manhattan. Eventually, in 1930s, he changed careers and began buying and managing residential real estate, succeeding again.

A new life had begun for him in America.

He married Shnorhig (Grace) Dadourian, who hailed from Marzevan, another city that had

Yervant Alexanian and his wife Shnorhig (Grace), later in life, in the United States.

suffered greatly during the genocide. Her older brother Vahram, who had intended to go to medical school, had also been conscripted into the Turkish Army during the war but had later fled to Russia and had married an Armenian woman. Her father, Harutyun, who was considered an activist and an advisor to the Armenian community and who was also the owner of a mill in Chavoush Kyugh, on the outskirts of Marzevan, had also been killed in the Genocide. In his role as advisor to the Armenian community in Marzevan, he met and consulted with Khrimian *Hayrig*[1] twice in his life. She, her mother Makrouhi (nee Arsenian), and her older sister Nevart had made their way to Istanbul, where her older sister established a dressmaking business. Her older sister was courted by a man named Garabed Nalbandian, living in Detroit, and she immigrated to America. Eventually, Shnorhig and her mother made their way to the United States, where they arrived, aboard the ship Conte de Savoia, on October 25, 1934. Shnorhig would later become an American citizen on June 3, 1941. She and her mother had first lived in Detroit with her older sister, but had since moved to New York. Edward (by which name Yervant was known in the United States) and Shnorhig (Grace) were introduced by a mutual friend and were married. By the time they got married, Shnorhig had become a respected dressmaker herself (she had run the shop in Istanbul after her sister's departure) and had worked for renowned stores such as Martha Shop, Bergdorf Goodman, and Tailored Woman. After marrying Yervant, she stopped working. She was also very active in Armenian life. She was a member of the Armenian General Benevolent Union (AGBU) Women's Guild, the Armenian Diocesan Auxiliary Guild, the Holy Cross Ladies' Guild, and the Armenian Evangelical Church Ladies' Guild. She held executive roles in many of these organizations. She was also a member of the AGBU Presidents' Club and the Armenian Assembly of America. The couple had one daughter—Adrienne G. Alexanian.

As his many letters and journals attest to, Alexanian became known as a family man, a community activist, and a mean backgammon player. He was a life member of the Armenian General Athletic Union, which he supported both morally and financially. He became a member of the AGBU Junior League on November 9, 1929, and was then inducted into the Bronx chapter in 1936, later becoming president of this chapter. He was a delegate to many AGBU conventions. Both he and his wife were gifted life memberships to the organization in 1970. Yervant was also a member of the Pan-Sebastia Rehabilitation Union, which he joined soon after landing in the United States in early 1920s. He later became the president of the New York chapter and would subsequently serve as an advisor to the organization, as well as on its executive committee. As a member of this organization, he was responsible for organizing many lectures and events relating to Sivas. He was also a delegate to the World Armenian Congress that was held in April and May of 1947 at the Waldorf Astoria in New York City.

Members of the Pan-Sebastia Rehabilitation Union in March 1921, in which Yervant Alexanian was a member. Alexanian's portrait is the fourth from the right, in the third row from the top.

He became a member of the Knights of Vartan, Vasbouragan Lodge, in 1955, and later served as the cocommander of the lodge. He personally sponsored the publication of a booklet about the organization and initiated the organization's involvement in yearly Armenian Genocide commemorations.

Alexanian was also the chairman of the Bronx committee for the raising of funds to build the St. Vartan Armenian Cathedral in New York and, after spending countless hours fundraising, was part of the groundbreaking ceremony.

He even offered to donate one of the buildings he owned in the Bronx to an Armenian nonprofit organization that wanted to build a school, as he wanted the Armenian language to remain alive and vibrant. This was one of the main causes he pursued. He was also instrumental in raising funds for the Armenian Language Lab, which was sponsored by the New York City Diocese of the Armenian Church in America. His contributions to this language lab were kept up after his death by his widow and his daughter.

All in all, throughout his life, he made financial contributions to the AGBU, the Armenian Apostolic Church, the Pan-Sebastia Union, as well as numerous American charities, such as Boys' Town and many medical charities.

He even corresponded with Metro-Goldwyn-Mayer studios, suggesting that they make a movie about the Armenian Genocide and his experiences throughout those dark years. He received a response, but the project was never realized.

Alexanian's philanthropic activities were not limited to the Armenian sphere. Feeling like he owed a debt of gratitude to the United States, he also wanted to contribute to other minorities in America. He bequeathed one of the buildings he owned in the Bronx to the National Association for the Advancement of Colored People.

Alexanian was also very generous with his family and friends. He helped many of his relatives financially, sent help to relatives of his wife who lived in Armenia, and worked with newcomers to America, finding them shelter, jobs, and sometimes even life partners. One of these men even appeared at his wake, sobbing and saying that Alexanian had "given him his life." Oftentimes, when the Pan-Sebastia Union received requests for financial assistance for new immigrants who needed help with basic necessities and had to deny them such help due to financial restraints, Alexanian would visit these folks personally and provide them support from his own pocket. He and his wife also donated generously to the Birds' Nest Orphanage[2] in Lebanon and received many letters of gratitude from the orphanage's director, Marie Jacobson.

Alexanian was often referred to as the *Tavloo King*, because he was a master backgammon player, and won many tournaments, organized by both Armenian and American groups and clubs.

After a lifetime of suffering, survival, service, and success, he died on February 1, 1983. At his funeral, representatives of many organizations, including the AGBU and Knights of Vartan, honored him in their own fashion. His wife survived him by thirteen years, dying on April 10, 1996.

Yervant Alexanian, later in life, with his wife and daughter.

The Edward Alexanian Fund at the AGBU supports Armenian Day Schools run by the AGBU and Armenian Day Schools run by the Mekhitarian Order across the United States. The Grace Alexanian Fund provides scholarships to Armenian students studying in various fields. The Edward and Grace Alexanian Fund at the Diocese of the Armenian Church of America also supports diverse events and publications, including many related to the recognition of the Armenian Genocide. The Edward and Grace Alexanian Fund at the Armenian Assembly of America supports advocacy for the recognition of the Armenian Genocide. In 2015, the Edward and Grace Alexanian Fund at the Diocese of the Armenian Church of America sponsored the publication of the program booklet distributed at the ecumenical service at the Washington Cathedral commemorating the 100th anniversary of the Armenian Genocide.

Notes

1. Mkrditch Khrimian, or Khrimian *Hayrig* (1820–1907), was the Armenian Patriarch of Constantinople, Prelate from the Van Area, and later Catholicos of All Armenians. He is renowned for his work to better the lot of Armenians living in the Ottoman Empire in the nineteenth century.
2. Sometimes referred to as the Danish Birds' Nest Orphanage, and still functioning to this day in Lebanon.

Final Thoughts

Every year on Mother's Day my memory goes back to July 3, 1915, the day when my mother kissed my eyes and said "goodbye my son, take good care of yourself." She was taking the road to forced deportation and starvation and I had to go back to the barracks to perform my military service for the regime that was sending my mother to her forced death with her eyes wide open. Oh, what a contrast! How I wish I knew which corner of the earth is keeping her innocent body so I could go there not only once a year but also every single day to shed my tears and kiss the ground that is keeping her. I never knew my father since I lost him when I was seven months old. It was her, my mother dearest of all mothers, who was left with eight orphans to raise...the eldest fourteen years old and the youngest me, seven months old. It takes a saint to perform miracles, and my mother was a saint.

Yervant Alexanian
May 14, 1953

Appendices

Appendix A:
Reflections of
Yervant Alexanian

In January 1954, with a group, I went to the United Nations building to participate in a guided tour. Just by coincidence, on that day, there was a meeting in one of the assembly rooms, scheduled for 10:30 a.m. The topic of the meeting was minorities, discrimination, and how to remedy such situations. Eleven nations had their representatives. I was not surprised to see that Turkey was not represented. I wonder if there are any minorities left within its borders . . . .

I went into the meeting as an observer. The participating members were arguing and passing resolutions that confirmed that small nations should also enjoy the same privileges in terms of travel and commerce as the big nations.

As I was coming out of the meeting, I approached one of the ushers and I asked if I could bring my case to this meeting and passing him the details, I said, "For three-and-a-half years I was an officer in the army of a country I served faithfully, the country in which I was born. I have in my possession all the documents that prove my story, as well as my honorable discharge papers. My question to this worthy meeting will be why is it that after my discharge I could not find my mother and relatives where I had left them."

The usher looked at me pensively and replied, "Are you Armenian? You have a very reasonable and just question, but this assembly does not entertain personal matters. If your claims and other similar ones are presented through a known organization I believe they will be put to discussion."

Where is the known Armenian organization to represent my case and those similar to mine? How are we to go through their channels? Is the time ripe to create one?

Here is another important question which should go through the channels of that organization: "What happened or who collected the insurance premiums,[1] the millions of dollars, belonging to the Armenians who were put to the death?"

It is a crime to kill, but to kill and then claim the insurance premiums of your crimes, that is unspeakable.

§§§

I was at a friend's house when I heard, on the Turkish radio hour, that on Wednesday, January 27, the president of Turkey, Celal Bayar, would arrive with his wife in New York. Then he was scheduled to fly to Washington to be the guest of our President for a few days. The announcer said that he would return to New York and hobnob with Greek, Jewish, and Turkish groups that were to host dinners at swanky hotels like the Plaza or the Waldorf Astoria.

In my opinion, protesting the Turkish president's visit is not what we want. It is high time we learn that the shedding of innocent blood does not mean a thing to those whose principal object is politics. What we need is to form a strong, united cooperation among different Armenian organizations, regardless of their denominational, political, or other affiliations to present our demands of restoration to the world's court, which is the United Nations Security Council. We must form one solid front.

I do not think there is enough money in the entire world to compensate for the terrible massacres and atrocities committed by the Turks during 1915–1920. Here is just one tiny example of those wrongdoings: In June 1915, I was called to serve in the armed forces of my country, Turkey, where I was born. I served as a soldier, as an officer, in various cities and places like Smyrna, Bandirma, the Dardanelles, Istanbul, and Sivas for a period of over three and a half years until December 1918, at which point I was honorably discharged. I remember all the dates and the locations of my service faithfully. I even had a couple of promotions to my credit. I have in my possession all the facts and documents to prove what I am saying. Now one simple question to the honorable Mr. President of Turkey—"what happened to my family while I was serving your country's military? Why could I not find them after I was discharged?" I am sure there are many like me here and they're asking the same simple question. From my immediate family, only three survived. What happened to the rest? Now I ask you, ladies and gentlemen—is this not worth investigating? Isn't this a supreme reason for us Armenians to form a united front with a solid demand for an explanation? How can anyone one forget an act so cruel and so barbaric?

I went down to the City Hall and watched the reception given in honor of the President of Turkey. It was amusing to see the presence of a handful of civilians. About half an hour before the appointed time, a young Turk began approaching the crowd and handed out free Turkish flags. Nobody accepted the offer, one person even made the comment "Look at that red flag, dyed with innocent Christian blood." "Not too different from the Communist flag," retorted another. Furthermore, nobody removed their hat when the band struck up the Turkish anthem, but of course, everyone did when they played the Star-Spangled Banner.

§§§

In my neighborhood, I met a Turk employed as the superintendent of a large building. He was in his early forties. When I first met him, he was delighted to find someone able to converse in Turkish. On one occasion, somehow the subject of the Armenian Genocide of 1915 came up. His response was *Kerenen Yonanla Yash da Yanar*, which means when the dry wood catches on fire, the wet wood will burn, too.

This man was not born yet in 1915, yet he knew the past, he knew what terrible injustices had occurred. He knew that in 1915 a terrible holocaust had been unleashed and had exterminated one-and-a-half million Armenians in a terrible, brutal way.

Reflections on the State of the Armenian Community

The Armenian nation is now divided. Due to some huge differences in opinion, due to serious ideological differences, and due to recent events, we have been split into factions.

Ultimately, what has happened is this—we are all the sons of the same family, and it is not acceptable for the sons of the same family to be butting heads. But the cold reality is that there is an "us and them" philosophy among many Armenians. It's not an Armenian phenomenon; it certainly exists in all nations, but we have been afflicted by it.

I speak specifically of Sivas Armenians. Sure, some of these divisions can be explained by people's ulterior motives, by vindictiveness, and by pettiness. However, whatever the motivations are, this causes division and internecine conflicts. There's barely a handful of us, and we still find a way to be at each others' necks. Back in the day, under the worst of circumstances, *Sebastatsis* of all walks of life used to unite to initiate events, to rebuild the ruined city, and to build hospitals, churches, schools, and orphanages in our homeland.

Now, due to the actions of the few, these initiatives are threatened. But these people are sorely mistaken if they think their personal affairs will get into the way of the reconstruction of our land.

Also, those who were born as Armenians, raised and educated as Armenians, simply call themselves friends of Armenia. We are not friends of Armenia! We are sons of Armenia. That statement encapsulates both our rights and our responsibilities. This is why we have been trying so hard to launch large-scale reconstruction efforts in the town in Armenia that bears the name of our beloved Sivas. The Armenian Diaspora must do this, must invest in Armenia.

After all, at least, we will then have the knowledge that those few Armenians who have found shelter in their own homeland will be living a decent life, with their lives, rights, and properties protected. This is the first duty of Diasporan Armenians. Their second duty is to keep the torch of their Armenian identities burning and to advocate for their homeland and their people in their countries of adoption. To keep our nation alive, to survive as Armenians, we must always be aware of our responsibilities.

November 21, 1934

Note

1. Alexanian is prescient here: in the early twenty-first century, successful class action suits would be brought against insurance companies in the United States and Europe for unpaid life insurance policies of Armenians massacred in the Genocide.

Appendix B:
Letters of Yervant Alexanian

Throughout his life in the United States, Alexanian wrote dozens of letters that were published in Armenian newspapers, as well as letters to dignitaries, including senators, ambassadors, and heads of states. The oldest of these letters is correspondence with Father De Lavernette, the headmaster of his old school in Sivas, which was written after the Armistice. The following is a selection of the many letters he sent and received, which shed additional life into Alexanian's thoughts and experiences.

With the exception of the letter from Pere De Lavernette, the letters below were originally written in English.

§§§

Letter from Father De Lavernette

1919
Adana

My dear Yervant,

I, too, was very happy to have received your news, and to know for sure that you are still among the living, as well as to have read in your letter of the survival of the many other of my friends in Sivas. I received your letter of June 12 only on July 11.

I have been receiving news of Sivas from M., a professor at the free school. Alas! How many lives lost among the teachers and the pupils! All we can do is remember the passion of Christ, who went through his sufferings without hatred and with dignity to help others, including those from Sivas who died. I myself am quite aware that I can count myself as a survivor. The day will come when we will meet again in Sivas, when it will be safe for us to return. Keep your courage. You are still young, and you will have time.

Adana suffered less than Sivas. Relatively speaking, there were few massacres and few deportations.

Please communicate my greetings to Kaloust, Kevork Khoriganian, and Hagop. I was very happy to hear of their news.

Please accept my fatherly sentiments and love, and my affections toward you.

Pere De Lavernette

Letter to Mr. Altemur Kilic, at the Turkish Embassy, Washington, D.C.

As an answer to your letter to the N.Y. Times of May 5, 1965, allow me to say that Ataturk's principles are only for the books, and they were not put to practice. Even strangers do not believe anymore that minorities are enjoying equal rights in his so-called republic. Visitors to Turkey will tell you so.

Had Turkey stayed neutral during World War I, today Turkey would be better off if not one of the richest countries in the world.

One wonders how it is that in this great country called America, everybody gets along regardless of color, nationality, or religion.

We are not trying to revive old, bitter memories. I for one am a survivor of that 1915 Genocide. I relive those memories every day of the week. The whole thing is very much alive to me and to other survivors. At least a dozen well-known foreign writers have published volumes as eye witnesses. Can anyone conceal a minaret in a sack?

Can anyone forget that in 1909 Talaat's life was saved by an Armenian who hid him in his house while he was wanted in Salonica? When Enver was wounded on the Russian Front, an Armenian soldier carried him on his back to safety. Yet these two ungrateful beasts planned to exterminate their saviors. Can anyone be so generous as to forget? Would you forgive and forget if all these things happened to you and to your family?

Mr. Kilic admits that this gifted people [the Armenians] contributed a great deal to Turkey's progress. We expect proof of appreciation, not by word, but by deed.

Yervant Alexanian
June 5, 1965

Letter to Michael Nalbandian, Yervant Alexanian's nephew

New York, December 22, 1971

Dear Michael;

If you go to Turkey, you must be diplomatic. Be friendly and try to mostly listen—don't say too much. Remember that your parents and family came to America before the Genocide—in 1912 or so.

Your father migrated from Erzincan. You'll have to find out from him precisely which neighborhood or street he hails from. As for your mother, Aunt Grace, her family was from Marzevon. Her father's mill was located in the Chavoush Kyugh (Chavoush Village). To get there from Marzevon you go Haji Kyugh, and from then on to Chavoush Kyugh. I believe you'll have to travel by beast to get there.

Incidentally, in order to make your way to Marzevon, I believe you have to through Sivas first, which is where I was born. I will try to give you the exact location of where we once lived. In Sivas, opposite the government building, there is a school called Sultaniyeh. Besides it, on a corner by a house, there was a steep hill. Our street was on the right side of that hill, and it was called Hassanli. About 260 yards down the street there is a fountain. Almost exactly opposite the fountain stood my uncle's house. In town, he was often called Terzi Serop Alexanian Oglu. See if this house still stands there.

Your mother and aunt have first cousins in France. Their names are Haykuhi, Berjouhi, and their brother Berge.

In Istanbul, too, they have first cousins. One of them is Haygaz Bingul Mosuklar. Also in Istanbul lives Hasmig's brother-in-law, Murad Dulgaroglu.

In Yerevan, they have a brother's wife, and also her son Zaven, who plays violin, and their daughter Melina, who plays the cannon.

When you decide to visit Turkey, again I advise you to be careful, just say that you wished to stop there on your way home. While there, be polite, diplomatic, and make believe that you are not familiar with the events of 1915. Be careful! While in Sivas you may also want to ask for the Bezirji Sokak Street, where there is a school whose building is made of stone. The Turkish school, Sultaniyeh, and the government building are also built of solid rock. I believe they are still there. Our street used to be part of the Konli Bogchi neighborhood.

We would like to receive a line or two from you wherever you travel. Of course, with the modern means of transportation, it will not take you long to get to places. You should know that in places like Sivas, Marzevon, and Yerevan, the winters can be quite cold. Make sure you pack sweaters, jackets, etc.

Also in Sivas, you may want to visit Terzi Suren Bankalar Jaddessi, who is a tailor. If you do, ask him about Bakal Nishan, my brother's brother-in-law. He is in the produce business, mainly buying and selling dry fruits from Malatya, southeast of Sivas.

We wish you all the luck, and stay healthy.

Yervant Alexanian

Letter to Michael Mgrditchian, who headed the Armenian General Athletic Union at the time

December 26, 1972
New York

Dear Mike,

Just a word of thanks for including me on your list of the AGAU Bulletin, which I receive regularly. Some of your articles take me way back to 1912 in the old country of Sivas. I remember when Boy Scouting was in its infancy, the Armenians school Aramian was the first one to organize a wonderful group under the leadership of the energetic Armenak Dumanian. They named it *Bartevagoump*. In a short period of time the group became the jewel of the athletic competitions. In a yearly contest they won first prize in soccer, group exercise, and the formation of human pyramids, atop of which a tiny Armenian boy hoisted the Turkish flag. What a beautiful gesture of their loyalty to Turkey.

A year later the French Jesuit Fathers' school organized our group, naming it Avant Guarde.

A few months later, the Turkish school Sultaniyeh organized their group and they called it Izji.

I remember in 1913 there was a contest of horse racing, bicycle racing, and wrestling. In the bicycle race, a young Armenian boy named Norshadian came first, winning a golden medal. He won it the hard way, as his bicycle had been damaged during the course of the race. He had stopped to repair the bike, and he had still been able to beat his closest rival, a Turkish lad.

All in all it is a common saying—healthy body, healthy mind. Our youth deserve very much to be supported in every possible way. Let us not sell them short.

It is a pity that the camp site committee that was organized in 1950 and worked quite hard did not eventually succeed. To this day, as you know, it is all still in the air. To my understanding, if it could be done, it should be done, and it must be done.

Wishing you all the energy to continue this very worthy enterprise for which you have gracefully volunteered. I remain very sincerely yours,

Edward Alexanian

Letter to the President of France

New York, March 31, 1973

Mr. Georges Pompidou
President de la Republique de France
Palais de L'Elysee, 55 Rue de Fauburg
Saint Honore 75008 Paris, France

Dear Mr. President,

November 5, 1913, is a day I shall never forget. On that day, at about noon, Father de Lavernette, Superieur du College des Quarante Martyrs in Sivas, Turkey, came to our classroom, followed by Mr. Avedis Semerdjian, his aide, to tell us that he had received orders from Mouammer (the governor of Sivas) to close the entire school and return to France with the rest of the fathers. We learned that the same order had been given to the sisters of the St. Joseph's order school, adjacent to ours.

Again I shall never forget his expression at that moment when emotion carried him away and he could not finish what he had to say.

Mr. Semerdjian told us to pack up our books and go home.

Furthermore, the governor's order was to pack up all of the schools' valuables into the four rooms on the top floor of a newly finished stone building which was used as living quarters for six of the teaching priests. Sivas had been proud of that building. The governor told the priests to seal the four doors with stamps, and promised that not even a needle would be missing when the fathers were allowed to return after the war. Alas, fewer than ten days after the departure of the good fathers, I saw with my own eyes the contents of the four rooms, including books, microscopes, electrical instruments, and the instruments of a complete brass band being carried away to the nearby Turkish school called Sultaniyeh, three blocks away from where we lived.

This is just an illustration, Mr. President, of how much one may trust the promises of the Turks.

The next day that I shall never forget is July 3, 1915. That was the day of the deportation of my family. I cannot describe the moment of separation. As orders were given for the deportation of the whole Armenian population in Sivas (which had been occupied by Turks for over six centuries), rumors were circulated that as the war was going on, the Turkish government wanted the Armenians to be removed to some safer places where they would be allowed to build their own communities. The remaining Armenians in town were to leave their homes and go without the male population, most of whom were in prison. The rest of this story is well known to the world—the ultimate result was the first massive genocide of the 20th century. In fact, the Armenians who were deported knew full well that their belongings would be confiscated by the government as soon as they were forced to leave—and so, before taking the road to deportation, they sold everything they had at ridiculously cheap prices, trying to get some cash for the road. My own family sold what we could, left most of our furniture with the Kapikian family, who were exempt from the deportation order, and left the rest of the items that we couldn't sell with our Turkish neighbors.

From my immediate Alexanian family, twenty persons perished from starvation, and many others died in unknown, cruel ways. They each died a thousand deaths, as an author once recognized. Adding to the above number, my uncles, their families, my aunts, and their families all perished. The overall death toll was 51 people.

When we witness that someone, somewhere stands up for justice, we must take pause. At this point, allow me to congratulate you, Mr. President, for the firm stand you took in allowing the erection of the monument which was long overdue, honoring the memory of our two million victims martyred during the First World War.

I, a miraculous survivor of that holocaust, remain respectfully yours,

Yervant Alexanian

P.S.: Enclosed you will find a photocopy of Father de Lavernette's letter sent to me in 1920, also copies of two prizes that I received—I call them my treasures. The card on the top right belongs to a French family for whom I worked as a shopper during my two-month summer vacations.

Letter to Dr. Richard Hovannisian, leading Armenian-American scholar of the Armenian Genocide

December 30, 1977

Dear Dr. Hovannisian,

Your lecture on the subject of accusing the writer of the *History of the Ottoman Empire and Modern Turkey* which I read in the Armenian Reporter's December 15, 1977 issue prompted me to write to you about my past experiences being the only survivor of my immediate family and fifty-four relatives from the 1915 Armenian Genocide.

I was born in Sivas on November 15, 1895. In 1915 I was drafted into the Turkish army's 27th *Kolordu* (Army Corps) workshop, first as a tailor and later I became the only bugler in the workshop. In 1916 I was sent to Istanbul with three other Armenians to be trained in the military school. I graduated as an officer and served in Smyrna, at the Dardanelles and various places. All in all I served three and a half years faithfully and I was honorably discharged when the Armistice was declared. I have all the official papers to verify my story. I also have the photographs of six other Armenian officers, including mine, in military uniforms. They also served faithfully for about the same length of time deprived of their parents and relatives.

I remember our teachers at the French Jesuit Fathers' School. They graduated previously from the same military school. Their names were Kachadour Fenerjian and Haroutyun Zaratzian. I do not have their photographs.

I have met Enver, the Minister of War, three times. I met him first when he went through Sivas on his way to the Russian Front. There he was wounded. He was carried away to safety from the battlefield by a Lieutenant Hovannes Aginian. As a reward his entire family was deported and perished. The second time I saw Enver was at the military workshop in Sivas, on an inspection tour. He was surrounded by high-ranking officers and accompanied by the Governor of Sivas. I met Enver for the third time in Melemon near Smyrna where I was in charge of the officers' *table d'hote*. This time he came in the company of Liman von Sanders and other high officers. They were there to inspect the 61st Division, which was assigned to replace the Division of the Dardanelles after the latter was torn to pieces in combat. I served *tan* to Enver Pasha and his group just before his special train pulled out of the station. He asked me, "Oh, are we to drink *tan*?" to which I replied, "It's just a farmer's treat . . . ." They did not stay for lunch.

Most of the survivors of the Genocide, especially those few that were accepted in the military school, were forced to become Muslims, and had to take on Turkish names. As I recall, in the fall of 1916, when the Russian Army, after capturing Yerzinga [modern-day Erzincan, Turkey], were only a couple of days from Sivas. Our commander at the military workshop, Isak Bey, gathered all the Armenians together and said:

"We have received strict orders not to allow anyone to survive with an Armenian name. You must immediately convert to Islam, or you must die." He added—"either you swallow the camel or you perish . . ."

This was shortly after they had collected three thousand young and old Armenian soldiers, who were meant to work building roads, and had massacred them somewhere outside of the City of Sivas. Some of my classmates had been among them.

At the beginning of the 1915 deportations, a prominent military officer had suggested that at least the families of those serving in the Army should be spared, but the infamous Governor Mouammer had argued that it was his business what should be done with the civilians.

I may add that after the signing of the Armistice and the allied battle-ships' arrival at the port of Istanbul, those that had converted to Islam immediately reverted back to their Armenian names. We all did so, and we had waited impatiently for a long time for the opportunity.

Of course every survivor's life story could form a volume. I made mine as brief as possible. Perhaps it's a story we could use to advance our cause, and to seek our rights and justice.

Very truly,
Edward Alexanian

P.S.: I have the group picture of the class 12 and also a group of teachers and students in machine gun training school taken in a suburb of Istanbul called Karshu Yaka.

Letter to the Armenian Assembly Oral History Project

February 8, 1978

Armenian Assembly Oral History Project
522 21st NW #120
Washington, D.C. 20006

Gentlemen,

I wish to submit my oral history about life in the Turkish army in which I served from 1915 to 1918, when the Armistice was declared to end the war.

I have the pictures of seven Armenian officers in uniform who graduated from Turkish military school. They also served faithfully, deprived from their families and relatives during the duration of the war.

I also have a unique picture of the whole graduating class #12, the only one of its kind. No other class had a picture taken.

I was born on November 15, 1895 in Sivas, Anatolia, where I witnessed many events. Among the worst of these events was seeing my family taking the road to forced deportation, a scene I shall never forget.

P.S.: I learned about this office in the Armenian Mirror-Spectator's January 28 issue.

Yervant Alexanian

Letter to the Armenian Reporter

New York, April 1978

Letter to the Armenian Reporter

This letter is in response to the findings of the article of the Istanbul Daily by Terjuman which you printed on the front page of the Reporter's January 20 issue saying that Talaat Pasha was not that bad after all. Terjuman admits that in 1915 there occurred the deportation of the Armenian nation which he mentions a few times, but he does not give any explanation as to the reasons or motivations, and doesn't explain why such a massive deportation should occur to the law-abiding, faithful citizens who had lived as subjects for over six centuries.

Is this the same Talaat that at one time boasted that in a short couple of months he had gotten rid of more Armenians than Sultan Hamid (also called The Red Sultan) had in more than 30 years during his regime?

Is this the same Talaat that went to the American ambassador Morgenthau and claimed the cash value of the insurance claims if his victims? The same Talaat who claimed himself as the sole beneficiary of those insurance claims?

Is this the same Talaat who claims that he gave orders to spare the families of those serving in the army, and to also spare the Catholic and Protestant Armenians? Then why is it that all of the Catholic inhabitants of the village of Perkenik near Sivas (famous as the birthplace of Daniel Varoujan) were some of the first to be deported, after their church had been burnt? As for Varoujan's fate, it is well-known how brutally he was killed.

Tarjuman needs to read the memoirs of the Catholic Archbishop Hovhanness Najlian, which describes how and where his flock of Catholic priests and nuns was put to the sword.

As for Armenian Protestants, the book of Protestant pastor Vatna Nartunian, Neither to Laugh Nor to Weep, will testify vividly as to how they were treated, and how many of them perished on the forced marches. This is just to mention one or two major publications on this subject. Several books were also published by foreign nationals, including Germans.

As for the transfer or protection of the material belongings of the deportees, ninety-five percent of what the Armenians had was left behind. There was no way of taking or carrying all their belongings, so most of them were moved to the Virgin Mary Cathedral in Sivas, and were thereafter auctioned off by the Turkish populace at the rate of five-ten Cents to the Dollar. A few years later that beautiful cathedral which had taken seven years to build was destroyed on the orders of the government.

As for Armenian soldiers' families, not a single family was spared except for well-known, essential artisans' families, and then only on the condition that they deny their Christian faith and become Muslims. Such as the case of another Armenian village called Tavra, also in Sivas. The inhabitants were expert flour mill operators. They were all forced to convert, then they were dispersed all over the country, sent wherever their skills were needed most.

In 1916, when the Russian Army captured Erzincan and it became quite apparent that in a few days they would advance on Sivas, there were over 3,000 Armenians serving in the armed forces, and they had been serving for two years, deprived of their families. They were imprisoned one night, and they were all massacred within a week's time.

One does not see anything in Terjuman's article except the irritation of a fifty-two year old wound.

Yervant Alexanian

Letter to Christopher J. Walker, British historian and author of volumes on Armenia's history

September 28, 1982

Dear Mr. Walker,

I thought it would be interesting to read about the 1915 Armenian holocaust, learning of it from a survivor and an eye witness.

As much as we do not need to approve of these Turkish officials being shot here and there, it is beyond understanding why the present Turkish regime denies the deportations and massacres. Many books by eye witnesses have disappeared from bookstores and colleges, destroyed by these official representatives. One should go, say, to the City of Sivas, where I was born, and take a look at the American Teachers' College (just completed in 1914), the elementary school, the French College of the Forty Martyrs, and many other Armenian school buildings and remaining churches, and ask the governing body what happened and where the students and staff are, and where the churchgoers are.

It would be impossible to forgive and forget unless some kind of justice is achieved with respect to the Armenian cause. Many nations smaller than Armenia have been granted independence. A nation that has had a glorious past like Armenia deserves consideration.

During the First World War, the Armenians were called the Little Entente. Armenian volunteers always took on the most dangerous tasks during that war and usually came out on the better side. But in the end, the Allies denied us our rights. When I was in Istanbul, I saw British, French, Italian, and American warships taking over the city. That was the perfect time for us to settle our cause. But the Turks outsmarted all of them, and were given Istanbul back.

Germany admitted her guilt, why isn't Turkey being forced to admit her guilt? How much harm could 2 million people do to a nation of 20 million Turks, fully mobilized and organized?

Yervant Alexanian

Correspondence with New York Senators
Robert Kennedy and Jacob J. Javits

When an official visit to the United States by Turkish President Cevdet Sunary was scheduled for April of 1967, Yervant Alexanian wrote to the two United States Senators from New York, Robert F. Kennedy and Jacob K. Javits, voicing his objection from his perspective as a survivor of the Armenian Genocide (see transcription above). At Alexanian's urging, both senators made inquiries with the Department of State, and shared the results with Alexanian in formal replies.

The following is the text of the letter he sent to both senators, followed by their responses.

§§§

Armenians throughout the world, and the one and a half million American citizens of Armenian heritage, mourn their martyred dead during the month of April—the month in which the 2 million victims of the first (and conveniently forgotten) Genocide of the 20th century were murdered by the Turks.

As law-abiding and tax-paying citizens, we have never objected to the use of our tax dollars when our government has extended loans to Turkey because we all realize that politics makes for strange bedfellows.

But now, one must speak up. It is unthinkable that you intend to add *insult to injury* by entertaining the President of Turkey during the month of April. April of all months of the year is set aside for prayers for our dead, commemorative programs, requiems, and other forms of remembrance, as well as the total absence of festivities.

Therefore, as one who is the survivor of the atrocities mentioned, I would like to say "never" for this particular state visit. But instead—being an understanding and loyal citizen of our beloved United States, I say:

ANY OTHER MONTH, BUT *NOT IN APRIL*

Thank you for your attention in this matter. His visit was postponed once because of President Johnson's illness. But please *not in April, not in April!!!*

Yervant Alexanian

Responses

The correspondence from Senators Kennedy and Javits, along with supporting documents from the United States Department of State, are reproduced here as facsimiles.

§§§

Reply from Senator Robert F. Kennedy, dated February 18, 1967, acknowledging the receipt of Alexanian's letter.

ROBERT F. KENNEDY
NEW YORK

United States Senate
WASHINGTON, D.C.

February 18, 1967

Mr. Edward Alexanian
2861 Creston Avenue
Bronx, New York 10468

Dear Mr. Alexanian:

Thank you very much for your letter of February 10.

I am looking into this matter at the present time, and I will be in further touch with you when I have additional information.

Thank you again for contacting me about this.

Sincerely,

Robert F. Kennedy

Follow-up reply from Senator Robert F. Kennedy, dated March 13, 1967, which included an enclosure, the response from the State Department regarding Kennedy's inquiry.

ROBERT F. KENNEDY
NEW YORK

United States Senate
WASHINGTON, D.C.

March 13, 1967

Mr. Edward Alexanian
2861 Creston Avenue
Bronx, New York 10468

Dear Mr. Alexanian:

Enclosed is a copy of the report I received in response to my inquiry in your behalf.

I hope this information is help-
ful to you, and that if I may be of
assistance in the future, you will feel
free to contact me.

Sincerely,

Robert F. Kennedy

Enclosure

Letter from the United States Department of State to Senator Robert F. Kennedy, enclosed in Kennedy's March 13, 1967 follow-up letter to Alexanian.

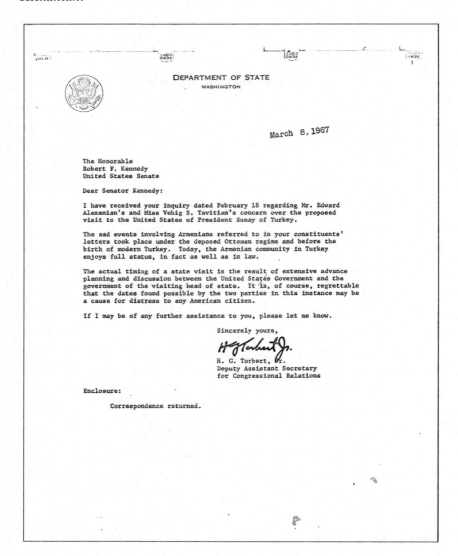

DEPARTMENT OF STATE
WASHINGTON

March 8, 1967

The Honorable
Robert F. Kennedy
United States Senate

Dear Senator Kennedy:

I have received your inquiry dated February 18 regarding Mr. Edward Alexanian's and Miss Vehig S. Tavitian's concern over the proposed visit to the United States of President Sunay of Turkey.

The sad events involving Armenians referred to in your constituents' letters took place under the deposed Ottoman regime and before the birth of modern Turkey. Today, the Armenian community in Turkey enjoys full status, in fact as well as in law.

The actual timing of a state visit is the result of extensive advance planning and discussion between the United States Government and the government of the visiting head of state. It is, of course, regrettable that the dates found possible by the two parties in this instance may be a cause for distress to any American citizen.

If I may be of any further assistance to you, please let me know.

Sincerely yours,

H. G. Torbert, Jr.
Deputy Assistant Secretary
for Congressional Relations

Enclosure:

    Correspondence returned.

Reply from Senator Jacob K. Javits, dated February 28, 1967, acknowledging the receipt of Alexanian's letter.

LISTER HILL, ALA., CHAIRMAN

WAYNE MORSE, OREG. JACOB K. JAVITS, N.Y.
RALPH YARBOROUGH, TEX. WINSTON L. PROUTY, VT.
JOSEPH S. CLARK, PA. PETER H. DOMINICK, COLO.
JENNINGS RANDOLPH, W. VA. GEORGE MURPHY, CALIF.
HARRISON A. WILLIAMS, JR., N.J. PAUL J. FANNIN, ARIZ.
CLAIBORNE PELL, R.I. ROBERT P. GRIFFIN, MICH.
EDWARD M. KENNEDY, MASS.
GAYLORD NELSON, WIS.
ROBERT F. KENNEDY, N.Y.

STEWART E. McCLURE, CHIEF CLERK
JOHN B. FORSYTHE, GENERAL COUNSEL

United States Senate

COMMITTEE ON
LABOR AND PUBLIC WELFARE

February 28, 1967

Mr. Edward Alexanian
2861 Creston Avenue
Bronx 68, New York

Dear Mr. Alexanian:

   Thank you for your letter of February 10 concerning the visit of the President of Turkey to the United States during the month of April.

   I am sending your letter protesting the visit of Turkey's President to the Department of State. When I have received the Department's comment I will be in touch with you again.

   With best wishes,

         Sincerely,

         Jacob K. Javits, U.S.S.

JKJ:lgb

Letter from the United States Department of State to Senator Jacob K. Javits, responding to his inquiry, and forwarded to Alexanian in a follow-up correspondence from Senator Javits.

DEPARTMENT OF STATE
WASHINGTON

Honorable Jacob K. Javits
United States Senate
Washington, D.C. 20510

Dear Senator Javits:

I have received your recent inquiry regarding Mr. Edward Alexanian's concern over the proposed visit to the United States of President Sunay of Turkey.

The sad events involving Armenians referred to in your letter took place under the deposed Ottoman regime and before the birth of modern Turkey. Today, the Armenian community in Turkey enjoys full status, in fact as well as in law.

The actual timing of a state visit is the result of extensive advance planning and discussion between the United States Government and the government of the visiting head of state. It is, of course, regrettable that the dates found possible by the two parties in this instance may be a cause for distress to any American citizen.

If I may be of any further assistance to you, please let me know.

Sincerely yours,

William B. Macomber, Jr.
Assistant Secretary for
Congressional Relations

Enclosure:

Correspondence returned.

Additional Noteworthy Correspondence

The previous letters are a selection of the ones Alexanian sent or received throughout his life. Below is an catalogue of additional important correspondence he engaged in, as well speeches he delivered and contributions he made to Armenian newspapers:

Letter to the Armenian Historical Research Society, dated September 17, 1968

In this letter, Alexanian offers a synopsis of his and his family's history for the archives of the Armenian Historical Research Society and suggests a united front of Armenian organizations and individuals who can take their cases to international courts.

Speech to the Knights of Vartan, undated

The Knights of Vartan are Armenian fraternal organizations, very similar to the Knights of Columbus. This speech, which seems to have been delivered to a full lodge, contains details of Yervant's experiences during the deportations, as well as before and after.

Letter to the Armenian Assembly Oral History Project, dated February 8, 1978

In this letter, Alexanian expresses his willingness to participate in the Oral History Project by contributing his experiences from 1915 through 1918. He states that he has a photograph of Armenian officers in the Ottoman Army from right before the Armistice. That photograph has been included in this work.

Letter to the Head of the Armenian Educational Council, undated

In this letter, Alexanian expresses his willingness to provide information for the *Armenian Reporter* regarding his experiences in the Ottoman Army and during the genocide.

I Survived, But . . .

Alexanian also wrote a series of articles for newspapers, titled *I Survived, But . . .* It seems like through these articles he wanted to communicate his experiences and thoughts to the newer generation. These articles provide details regarding his experiences during the Genocide, as well as before and after.

Appendix C: Documents of Yervant Alexanian (Facsimile with English Transcript/Translation)

Certificate from the College Des Quarante Martyrs

Dated November 9, 1912, this document certifies to Yervant's satisfactory performance in school.

Certificate Attesting to Attendance of the Quarante Martyrs School

The document, signed by the Superior of the Fathers of the Armenian Mission in Constantinople, certified that Yervant Alexanian was a student at the Quarante Martyrs College in Sivas, where he spent seven years, and was on the point of finishing his studies when war erupted. The Father Superior also attests that his performance as a student was satisfactory.

Ottoman Identification Document for Yervant Alexanian
Contrasted with below document, which is his identification document after he
converted and changed his name

Ottoman State
Ministry of the Interior
Name: Yervant son of Alexan
Father's name: Deceased
Mother's name: Hnazant
Date and place of birth: 1312 Hijri (1895), Sivas
Religion (millet): Armenian
Marital status: He has no wife
Height:
Skin color:
Province (Vilayet): Sivas
Place of residence: Bazar seqtor
House number: 35
Residence kind: House (khan)
(Officiating officer's seals and signature)
Issued in: 1320 Hijri (1904)

Ottoman Identification Document for Yusuf Zia Effendi

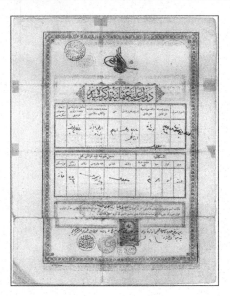

Ottoman State
Ministry of the Interior
Name: Yusuf Zia
Father's name: Abdullah
Mother's name: Amineh
Date and place of birth: 312 Hijri [1896] at Rumi Azanikli
Religion [millet]: Islam
Marital status: Has no wife
Height: Long
Skin: Tanned
Province [Vilayet]: Sivas
Place of residence: Bazar sector
House number: 35/2
Residence kind: house [khan]
Officiating officers seals and signature
Issued in: 1915

Military Booklet of Reserve Officers' School for Yusuf Zia Effendi

[Handwriting: Belongs to Yusuf Zia, son Of Abdullah, serial number 1388/12]
[Photo of individual with the school's official seal partially covering photo]
[Page 2]
Officer's Specialization: Accounting official
Rank: Reserve Officer
Name: Yusuf Zia Effendi
Father's Name: Abdullah
Place of Birth: Sivas
Date of Birth: 1312 Hijri [1896]
Army Corp.: Sivas, Military Corp.
Entry date: November 4, 1332 Hijri [1916]
Study classification: completed Study course "B" in 1916
[Page 3]
Current Situation:
Serial Number: 1388/12
Since he has graduated from the Sivas abovementioned Military Academy by completing the course assigned to him, He is able to serve his country and has had no negative points as to his character. This entry has been recorded at this time based upon the individual's performance.
[Page 4-12]
Course description
[Military academy's official circular seals and proper signatures]

Official Document of Release from Duty and Remaining as a Reservist Officer for Yusuf Zia Effendi

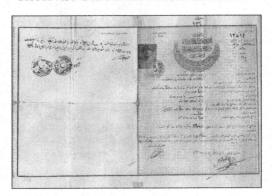

From volume 126
Personal File Number: 815
[Photo of military person with official seal partially covering photo]
Serial Number: 12514
Name: Yusuf Zia
Father: Abdullah
From: Sivas
Born: 1896
Place and date of Birth: Sivas, 1896
Place of Residence: Yankili, Street 30, house number 20
Place residing after joining army: . . .
Military corp. serving in and date admitted: Sivas military corp., since 1917
Was Military file sent to headquarters: yes
Case files serial number: 23513
Education before entering Military: graduate of secondary school
When was documentation started and to whom directed: in 1917 and was directed to first place of military service
What military section was person serving in: 61st battalion
What date candidate rose to officer status: April 22, 1917
[Official seals and signatures of military sections and headquarters. Dated May 12, 1918]
The military officer, Yusuf Zia Effendi, was released from the military and was regarded to be in the reserve forces as of November 2, 1919, per the recommendations of his superiors given on March 16 and 29, 1919.
Seal and signature of official military authority

Membership Application to the Armenian Officers' Association

<Marked at the very top with "infantry".>

Number # 10

Name and birthplace: Yervant Nishan Alexanian, Sivas

Date of birth: 1896, registered as 1312 of the Muslim calendar

Education: In Sivas, and in the Forty Martyrs' College

Military rank: officer's candidate

Foreign languages: French and Turkish

Marital status: single

In which army have you served, and for what duration? For a year and a half in the 10th workshop as a tailor, then was sent to the military institute ad after graduating, served in the 61st (*Frkat Tehjizat Melbasat*). I was eventually made officer of procurements, <ILLEGIBLE>

Did you participate in combat? See above

Biographical Sketches: I attended the French College of Sivas for seven years. As soon as I entered my last year there, war was declared. Thus, I was not able to graduate. Soon after that, I was called up to the army, and conscripted as a military tailor in the 10th Division's workshop. A month later, the town's Armenians were deported and I was separated from my family and friends. I have still not found them. After staying at the workshop for a year and a half, Armenian soldiers who were building a road nearby were massacred. Just after that I was told that my only salvation lay in converting to Islam. I was forced to become an apostate. Sometime later, I was transferred to Istanbul, to the officer's school. After finishing my studies, I was stationed with the 61st Division, as a procurement officer, responsible for their food supplies and uniforms. I served there for six months. I was still considered an unarmed officer at the time. I then received a new order, and received an additional six months of infantry and 2 months of artillery officer's training. I thus became an armed member of the forces. Just as I was about to be deployed to the front, the Armistice was declared and I was discharged. I never became a full officer, as I was discharged before my final promotion went through.

Patriarchate Claims Reports

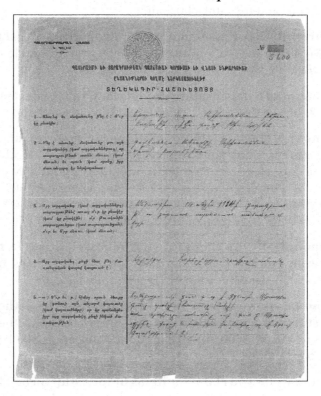

Armenian Patriarchate
Constantinople
Claims Report—Presented by Families that Suffered Material Damages
During the War and the Deportations—Claims number 5600

Name, Surname, and Address: Yervant Nishan Alexanian, Peria, Building of the Bankalt Building, Street Number 40/62.

Name and Surname of Your Kin who were Killed During the Events, and whose Inheritances you Claim: Hovhanness Alexanian, Serop Alexanian, Misak Parseghian.

Where did your relatives live before the deportations? When were they deported or killed?: Deported from Sivas, May 14, 1914, and killed at unknown locations.

What is your relationship to the relatives you named: They were my brother, uncle, and my aunt's husband.

Who Currently has Possession of the Properties or Estates you Claim: My uncle owned a house in Sivas. My aunt's uncle owned a home on Bekmez Street, as well as a half of a shop.

What amount of compensation do you claim for the deaths of your relatives?: I leave this to the discretion of the Patriarchate.

What amounts do you claim for clothing, accessories, and money that was stolen from your relatives?: My brother—clothing, 600 Pounds; accessories, 140 Pounds; money, 250 Pounds. My uncle—clothing, 800 Pounds; accessories, 180 Pounds; money, 600 Pounds. My aunt's husband—clothing, 700 Pounds, accessories, 60 Pounds; money, 700 Pounds. A total of 4030 Pounds.

What amounts do you claim for your relative's losses in terms of furniture: my brother—300 Pounds, my uncle—500 Pounds, my aunt's husband—500 Pounds. A total of 1300 Pounds.

What amounts do you claim for items confiscated from these individuals' stores and commercial establishments?: my brother—1200 Pounds; my uncle—1600 Pounds; my aunt's husband—300 Pounds. A total of 3100 Pounds.

What amounts do you claim for items or foodstuff owned by these relatives that were spoiled or destroyed after the deportations: my brother—200 Pounds; my uncle—350 Pounds; my aunt's husband—80 Pounds. A total of 630 Pounds.

How much do you claim for losses of income for these relatives?: from the beginning of the war up to the Armistice—my brother—400 Pounds; my uncle—900 Pounds; my aunt's husband—1200 Pounds. A total of 2500 Pounds.

A total of 11560 Pounds.
Date—Constantinople, October 26, 1920.

Notes: These sums were calculated using monetary evaluations at the start of the war. Aside from the relatives mentioned, my family lost many other individuals, for whom I also claim compensation.

Second Patriarchate Claims Report

Armenian Patriarchate
Constantinople
Claims Report—Presented by Families that Suffered Material Damages
During the War and the Deportations—Claims number 6614

Name and surname: Yervant Nishan Alexanian

Where did you live before the deportations? Where do you live now? Sivas. Now I live in at number 40/62 of Bakaght Street.

What immovable properties did you own? What sums do you claim? In whose hands are they currently? Three fields, 1 mill stone. Located in Sivas, currently appropriated by local Turks. A total sum of 800 Ottoman Pounds.

Furniture, clothing, and possessions: Furniture: 500 Ottoman Pounds, clothing: 450, jewelry: 60, movable items: 120. Total: 1130 Ottoman Pounds.

Loss of income: for three and a half years: 105 Ottoman Pounds.

Farming items, seeds, and grains: seeds: 40 Ottoman Pounds, roots: 50, grains: 25. Total: 115 Ottoman Pounds.

TOTAL BALANCE: 2150 Ottoman Pounds

Valuations in this form are based on pre-war currency exchange rates.

Missak Missirian fils
Tabacs en feuilles

Adresse télégraphique:
Missirian-Bruxelles

Bruxelles le 4th March 1921.
102, Rue du Marais.

Téléphone Bruxelles 2399.

CERTIFICATE

We hereby certify that Mr Yervant ALEXANIAN has been employed in 1919/1920, about one year, by our Constantinple Agency, as bookkeeper and also for all kinds of accounts, for tobacco purchases, shipments, etc.

We have always been very satisfied with his work.

Employment Certificate

Pass from British High Commissioner

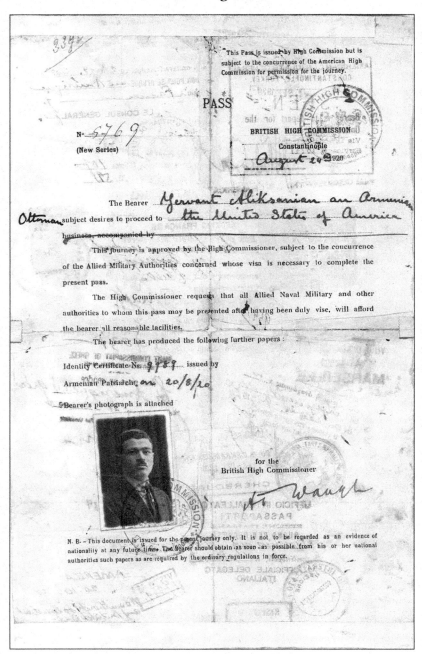

Pass Number 5769 (New Series)

British High Commission
Constantinople
August 24, 1920

The bearer, Yervant Aliksanian (sic), an Armenian Ottoman subject desires to proceed to the United States of America.

This journey is approved by the High Commissioner, subject to the concurrence of the Allied Military Authorities concerned whose visa is necessary to complete the present pass.

The High Commissioner requests that all Allied Naval Military and other authorities, to whom this pass may be presented after having been duly vise (sic), will afford the bearer all reasonable facilities.

The bearer has produced the following further papers:

Identity Certificate No. 9989 issued by Armenian Patriarch, as August 8, 1920

Bearer's photograph is attached.

Vaccination Documents

These were probably presented to the British High Commissioner alongside the application for passage to the USA.

Armenian document—Dr. Keklikian certifies that Yervant Alexanian of Sivas, aged 25, does not currently suffer from any illness.

French document—Dr. Karateve certified that Yervant Alexanian (sic), aged 24, does not suffer from Trachoma. Dated December 10 1920.

Immigration Documents

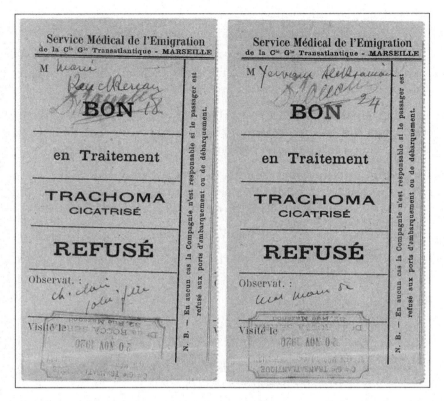

Yervant's and Marie's trachoma vaccination certifications, received in Marseilles.

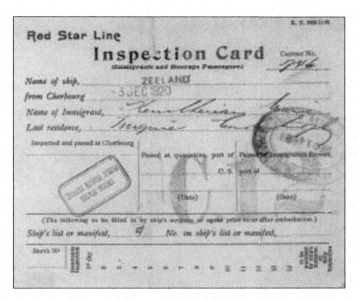

Red Star Line, Inspection Card, number 1746. Name of ship: Zeeland. This was for Marie Keushkerian, and it is dated December 3, 1920. Last residence is marked "Turquie," or Turkey in French. Inspected and passed at Cherbourg. Manifest number 7 on the ship.

Timeline of Yervant N. Alexanian

Birth: November 15, 1895, Sivas, Turkey

Death of father: June 12, 1896

Closure of school: November 5, 1914

Begins working at Hajinlian's store: November 10, 1914

Arrests begin in Sivas: June 3, 1915

Conscription into the Ottoman army: June 10, 1915

Deportation orders arrive: June 15, 1915

First neighborhood in Sivas deported: June 22, 1915

Deportation of his neighborhood: July 3, 1915

Honorably Discharged from the Ottoman army: December 20, 1918

Departure from Istanbul: October 27, 1920

Arrival in Marseilles: November 2, 1920

Departure from Cherbourg: December 3, 1920

Arrival in New York: December 13, 1920

Select Bibliography and Further Reading

Books on the Armenian Genocide

Akçam, T. *A Shameful Act: The Armenian Genocide and the Question of Turkish Responsibility*. New York: Holt, 2006.

Balakian, G. *Armenian Golgotha: A Memoir of the Armenian Genocide, 1915–1918*. Translated by P. Balakian and A. Sevag. New York: Vintage, 2009.

Cheterian, V. *Open Wounds: Armenians, Turks and a Century of Genocide*. London: C. Hurst, 2015.

Dadrian, V. *The History of the Armenian Genocide*. New York: Berghahn, 2003.

Der Matossian, B. *Shattered Dreams of Revolution: From Liberty to Violence in the Late Ottoman Empire*. Stanford: Stanford University Press, 2014.

de Waal, T. *Great Catastrophe: Armenians and Turks in the Shadow of Genocide*. Oxford: Oxford University Press, 2015.

Kevorkian, R. *The Armenian Genocide: A Complete History*. London: I.B. Tauris, 2011.

Hovannisian, R. *The Armenian Genocide in Perspective*. New Brunswick: Transaction, 1987.

Morgenthau, H. *Ambassador Morgenthau's Story: A Personal Account of the Armenian Genocide*. Garden City: Doubleday, 1918.

Nakashian, A. *A Man Who Found a Country*. New York: T.Y. Crowell, 1940.

Robertson, G. *An Inconvenient Genocide: Who Now Remembers the Armenians?* London: Biteback, 2015.

Stone, D. "Holocaust Testimony and the Challenge to the Philosophy of History." In *Studies in Social and Political Thought, 2: Social Theory after the Holocaust*, edited by R. Fine and C. Turner, 219–34. Liverpool: Liverpool University Press, 2000.

Svazlian, V. *The Armenian Genocide. Testimonies of the Eyewitness Survivors*. Yerevan: Gitutiun, 2011.

Torossian, S. *From Dardanelles to Palestine: A True Story of Five Battle Fronts of Turkey and Her Allies and a Harem Romance*. Boston: Meador, 1947.

Üngör, U., and M. Polotel. *Confiscation and Destruction: The Young Turk Seizure of Armenian Property.* London: Continuum, 2011.

Virabyan, A., ed. *Armenian Genocide by Ottoman Turkey, 1915: Testimony of Survivors, Collection of Documents.* Yerevan: Zangak, 2013.

Books on the City of Sivas

Gapikian, G. *Eghernapatum [History of Genocide: An Account of the Deportations and Massacres of the Armenians of Sebastia and Lesser Armenia].* Post'ěn: "Hayrenik"'i Tparan, 1924.

Hovannisian, R., ed. *Armenian Sebastia/Sivas and Lesser Armenia.* Costa Mesa: Mazda, 2004.

Nat'anean, P. V. *Teghekagrut'iwn endhanur vichakin Sebastioy* [General Survey of the Sebastia Diocese]. Constantinople Armenian Patriarchate, 1877.

Natanyan, B. *Sivas 1877.* Turkey: Birzamalar Yayıncılık, 2007. (In Turkish)

Oskean, H. H. *Sebastioy vank'ere* [Monasteries of Sebastia]. Venetik: S. Ghazar, 1946.

Patrik, A. N. *Patmagirk' Hushamatean Sebastioy ev gawari hayut'ean* [History Memorial Book of Armenians of Sebastia and Its District], 2 vols. Peyrut': Tp. Mshak, 1974.

Sebastats'i, H. *Patmut'iwn Sebastioy* [History of Sebastia]. Erevan: Haykakan SSH GA Hratarakch'ut'yun, 1974.

About the Author and Contributors

Yervant Alexanian (1895-1983), born in Sivas, Turkey, survived the Hamidian massacres as an infant to later fight for survival as a conscript in the Ottoman Turkish Army during the Armenian Genocide of 1915. He fled to America in 1920, where he spent his life advocating justice for his people.

Adrienne G. Alexanian (Editor) has spent years preparing her father's manuscript for publication, to carry forward his life's work, and bring his story of survival and advocacy to the attention of the world. She is an educator, having received her bachelor's and master's degrees from Hunter College, and is a 2010 recipient of the Ellis Island Medal of Honor.

Simon Beugekian (Translator) a graduate of Northeastern University, was born in Greece, grew up in Lebanon, and resides in California. He has translated *Goodbye Antoura: A Memoir of the Armenian Genocide* as well as screenplays and documents of historical importance.

Israel W. Charny (Foreword) is the Executive Director of the Institute on the Holocaust and Genocide in Jerusalem, past editor of the award-winning *Encyclopedia of Genocide* (2000), and author of *The Genocide Contagion* (2016).

Sergio La Porta (Introduction) is the Haig and Isabel Berberian Professor of Armenian Studies at California State University, Fresno. He lectures on the Armenian Genocide in the "Holocaust and Genocide Lecture Series" at Sonoma State University (since 2010), and was president of Fresno's Armenian Genocide Centennial Committee (2013-2015).

§§§

CPSIA information can be obtained
at www.ICGtesting.com
Printed in the USA
LVOW13*1617041017

551167LV00013B/224/P